FIT TO RUN

THE COMPLETE GUIDE TO INJURY-FREE RUNNING

FIT TO RUN

THE COMPLETE GUIDE TO INJURY-FREE RUNNING

PHILLIP PEARSON

THE CROWOOD PRESS

First published in 2014 by
The Crowood Press Ltd
Ramsbury, Marlborough
Wiltshire SN8 2HR

www.crowood.com

British Library Cataloguing-in-Publication Data
A catalogue record for this book is available from the British Library.

ISBN 978 1 84797 701 4

Frontispiece: Graham Hillditch

Dedication
To my wife, Christine, Adult Beginners Coach at East Cheshire Harriers & Tameside Athletic Club, who has helped so many new runners to progress safely through the coaching system and eventually complete their first race. Thanks for her support and assistance with this book.

Acknowledgements
I would like to thank the following individuals who have helped towards the completion of this book: Christine Pearson, ECH & TAC Adult Beginners Coach, for her assistance, advice and contributions; Bob Smith, former lecturer in Physical Education, Sports Science and Recreation Management at Loughborough University, for allowing the use of his original concept of the cardio-respiratory system compared to a railway transport system; Sabine Kussmaul for her 'train' illustrations in Chapter 6; Tracy Potts for demonstrating a number of stretching exercises. Thanks are also due to Consulting Editor, Dr Wendy Dodds, for her advice and contributions. Wendy has been a Sports Physician for over thirty years, a Team GB doctor at four Olympic Games, and most recently, a volunteer doctor at London 2012. In retirement she has found the time to compete as a full-time athlete, allowing her to reproduce times from twenty years ago when training was limited by professional commitments.

Typeset by Jean Cussons Typesetting, Diss, Norfolk

Printed and bound in India by Replika Press Pvt Ltd

CONTENTS

INTRODUCTION

This book is for runners of all standards, whether complete beginners aiming to increase health-related fitness and weight control, or experienced club runners competing in distance races of five, ten, twenty kilometres, or a full marathon.

Any exercise programme should be based on scientific principles and participants should have some knowledge of the body, how it works, how it responds to training and what can go wrong.

Running is a very accessible and inexpensive form of aerobic conditioning. All that is needed is a suitable pair of running shoes, appropriate clothing and the courage to step out of the front door.

The human body is designed to run. Our earliest ancestors ran great distances in order to survive, hunting to eat, often out-running their quarry until it became exhausted. They would even have had to run to avoid becoming prey. Had they not been designed to run, and able to run, they would not have survived. Mankind would have died out and we would not be here today.

Over many millennia, and because of ever-increasing labour-saving technology, man has eliminated the need to run and body structures have weakened, especially the feet (see more about the structure and function of the human foot in Chapter 7).

Running injuries occur because of the body's reliance on artificial devices, which try to compensate for weaknesses in tissues subjected to too much stress too soon.

Our bodies are basically the same as early man and we are still designed to run, despite what the sceptics might say. Those who preach the 'dangers' of running usually do so out of personal belief, not backed up by scientific evidence, research or study. The benefits of running far outweigh the hazards.

Running provides many health-related benefits, such as:

- **Cardio-protection** – Running, as a form of aerobic conditioning exercise, strengthens the heart muscle (myocardium); it helps to lower and control blood pressure and increases levels of good cholesterol (HDL).

- **Muscle tone** – Running strengthens and tones skeletal muscle, making everyday tasks easier and potentially improving posture.

- **Bone strength** – Running is weight-bearing exercise that increases bone density and bone strength.

- **Weight control** – Running increases calorie expenditure and can assist with weight reduction and weight control, which in turn can contribute towards cardio-protection.

- **Relief from stress** – Running increases the secretion of mood-enhancing hormones known as endorphins, chemicals which affect the brain to bring about a more relaxed state of mind.

- **Social wellbeing** – Although sometimes it can be pleasant to run by yourself, alone with your thoughts, it may be more interesting to run with another person, not only for social interaction (for maximum aerobic benefit you should be running at a pace whereby you can maintain a conversation), but also as a safety precaution, especially for women who might feel vulnerable alone on dark nights, in open countryside or parkland.

The term **prevention of running injuries** may be a misnomer: it is not possible to prevent injury. Injuries can happen despite the best precautions. What we can do, however, is reduce the *risk of injury*. This requires a degree of knowledge – an awareness of correct warm-up and essential cool-down, the importance of stretching for muscle suppleness and joint flexibility, the development and maintenance of core strength and stability, the development of a recommended running technique, an awareness of current fitness level, appropriate intensity and progression, and a knowledge of how the body adapts to exercise and training.

The information, suggestions and recommendations offered in this book are advisory and are based on scientific knowledge, research and many years' experience. It should therefore be understood that the author and publishers carry no liability.

Running for Fitness and Fit to Run

What do we mean by 'fitness'? Many authorities have attempted to define the meaning of fitness. Sharkey (1990) spoke of both aerobic and muscular fitness. He defined aerobic fitness as the capacity to take in, transport and utilize oxygen, developed and maintained through large-muscle activities such as walking, jogging, cycling, swimming, and other activities that allow sustained metabolism. For muscular fitness he included strength, muscle endurance and flexibility.

Cullum and Mowbray (1989) spoke of total fitness, which includes physical, nutritional, medical, mental, emotional and social fitness. They defined total fitness as the ability to meet the demands of the environment, plus a little in reserve for emergencies. They defined physical fitness as the capability of the heart, blood vessels, lungs and muscles to function at optimal efficiency.

Hazeldine (1992) wrote that fitness refers to the total dynamic physiological state of the individual, ranging on a continuum from optimal human performance to severe debilitation and death.

Honneybourne *et al.* (1996) described fitness simply as the ability to cope effectively with the stresses of everyday life.

Glover *et al.* (1996) stated that physical fitness implies optimal functioning of all physiological systems of the body, particularly the cardiovascular, pulmonary and musculo-skeletal systems.

Fit for What?

It is generally considered that there are two types of fitness: **general fitness** (or health-related fitness) and **specific fitness** (sometimes referred to as sport-related, skill-related, or task-related fitness).

General or health-related fitness involves the development of *strength, stamina,* and *suppleness* (referred to as the three 'S's).

Specific fitness builds on the three S's

and involves the development of factors such as skill, speed, power, agility, balance and co-ordination. Depending on the sport, activity or task to be performed on a regular basis, a level of health-related fitness should first be developed and then any of those extra factors. This supports the well-known adage that a person should get fit to play sport, not play sport to get fit.

We can apply this adage to the novice runner: don't run to get fit – get fit to run.

After a comparative sedentary lifestyle, do not expect to be able to set off for a couple of miles of jogging. Prepare in advance with a few weeks of regular, good-paced walking. After that, progress to walking interspersed with short intervals of jogging. Gradually, over a period of time, increase the length of the jogging intervals and decrease the walking. Eventually, with patience and careful progression, the walking sections can be omitted and a considerable distance can be run.

> Jogging and running are basically synonymous, but jogging tends to suggest a slower pace (e.g. more than nine minutes per mile), whereas running suggests a faster pace (e.g. less than nine minutes per mile).

FITNESS

GENERAL or HEALTH-RELATED FITNESS

STRENGTH
STAMINA
SUPPLENESS

SPECIFIC FITNESS

SPEED
SKILL
POWER
AGILITY
BALANCE
CO-ORDINATION

Strength is defined as the ability for/of a muscle or muscles to exert a force to overcome a resistance. It is increased by working muscles against progressively increasing resistances greater than those to which they are accustomed. Under the heading of strength, in the context of health-related fitness, we could also include muscular endurance and muscle tone.

Muscular endurance is the ability for muscles to contract for longer periods of time against lighter resistances (and to resist fatigue).

Muscle tone is a healthy condition of the muscle and its connection with the nervous system; the muscle is in a state of continuous stimulation and semi-contraction, ready to work.

Stamina in this context refers to cardiorespiratory endurance: the development of the cardiovascular and respiratory systems and their ability to transport and supply oxygen to the tissue cells of the body, particularly to the cells of the working muscles.

Suppleness strictly refers to a condition of the muscles whereby they are able to lengthen effectively and therefore allow flexibility at the joints (flexibility means range of movement [ROM] at joints). In the context of health-related fitness suppleness is synonymous with flexibility (being a more suitable word to provide the three S's).

There can be an amount of overlap between general (health-related) fitness and specific fitness. Factors such as balance and co-ordination are important attributes in everyday life and will most likely be developed to some degree through health-related exercise.

Specific fitness factors may have to be developed in order to perform particular sports or tasks; to be able to run a marathon a person would first have to develop a level of general fitness (stamina, strength and suppleness), but would have to specifically increase stamina to a high level. Some degree of strength would occur in the particular muscles used in running, but this strength would plateau out. A high degree of flexibility may not be a vital factor in distance running, but suppleness of the muscles involved will assist stride length and may reduce the risk of overuse injury. We could argue that running involves some degree of skill which has to be acquired through regular practice.

Development of the three S's, and therefore development of a degree of general fitness, can reduce health risks; thus the term 'health-related fitness'. Regular, moderate to vigorous exercise such as running can/may increase immunity to disease and reduce the likelihood of chronic conditions such as coronary heart disease (CHD).

Many studies, articles and books have shown the importance of regular exercise as a preventative factor in the development of chronic conditions and diseases. However, excesses of training can result in injury, a suppressed immune system and susceptibility to viral infections.

Can fitness be measured? Yes it can, but we must first define fitness so that we can determine exactly what it is we are measuring. Fitness assessments (or tests) are carried out on a regular basis in health clubs, university research laboratories and sports science laboratories to assist athletes and sports people with their training.

The American doctor Kenneth Cooper, credited as being the father of aerobics (meaning the development of aerobic capacity), considered the main factor which determined whether or not a person was fit was their aerobic capacity, or how well the body could take in and use oxygen to produce energy. Therefore we could conclude that stamina has an important place in the definition of fitness, although strength and suppleness are also very important factors for all-round fitness.

With the athlete or sports person many specific measurements may be taken and may be of value. Also in a health-related fitness test a number of specific tests may be performed, such as blood pressure, lung function (one element of which is peak expiratory flow [PEF]), percentage body fat, and flexibility, which provide information regarding the physical condition of the subject. However, if we consider Dr Cooper's definition of fitness, then the one measurement carried out which could truly be considered a measurement of fitness is when we measure a person's aerobic capacity.

To measure aerobic capacity we measure maximum oxygen uptake (VO_2 Max). This is the maximum volume of oxygen which can be extracted from the atmosphere, supplied to, and taken up by the tissue cells per minute. It may be expressed as litres per minute (L/min) or as millilitres per kilogram of body weight per minute (ml/kg/min). (See Chapter 5.)

Our running should be performed in a way that is safe, effective and enjoyable, to develop life-long health and fitness. We are exercising for health-related reasons, to develop and maintain a level of fitness which promotes a healthy state in the body.

Fitness and health are not the same. We have already defined fitness earlier in this section. Health may be defined as 'freedom from disease'. A certain level of physical fitness can promote health by enhancing the immune system, making us more resistant to infection. It improves all systems of the body to reduce the development of chronic conditions such as heart disease, obesity and high blood pressure. Even the highly competitive distance runner may be advised to consider long-term health and fitness and not just short-term fitness for a comparatively brief sporting career.

Cross-training can have a profound influence on reducing the risk of injury through over-training and overuse. As well as days off from running for rest and recovery, activities such as swimming or cycling could be performed as an occasional alternative to running. In addition, it can be very beneficial to perform core stability exercises regularly (see Chapter 8).

With knowledge of the body, its structure and function, the scientific principles of training, and of safe running technique, our aim can be achieved – to enjoy our running with a minimal risk of injury.

CHAPTER 1

THE BASIC PRINCIPLES OF EXERCISE AND TRAINING

All those involved in regular exercise and training, especially runners, should be aware of certain basic principles in order that exercise programmes are safe and effective. To reduce the risk of injury, regular runners, or anyone wishing to take up running, should be aware of how the body reacts to the stresses imposed by the activity.

The body thrives on physical stress. Physical stress is necessary for the development and maintenance of healthy tissue, and for that tissue to strengthen and improve its function.

Every exercise and training programme must be based on the scientific principles known as **Training Principles**. The following principles apply to the development of all systems of the body and all fitness factors.

The Five Training Principles

Overload: In order for the systems of the body to become more effective (fitter/ stronger) they must be subjected to greater physical stress than that to which they are accustomed. Such physical stress is known as overload. Exercise overloads the skeletal, muscular, cardiovascular, respiratory and nervous systems.

Adaptation: Over a period of time, following repeated bouts of overload, anatomical and physiological changes (adaptations) occur in the tissues so that they become more able to handle the increased stress. In other words, they become fitter and stronger and the level of stress to which they have been subjected is now considered normal.

Progression: If further increases in fitness and strength are required, further overload must be applied. The systems of the body must be stressed further, or worked harder. It is important that progression is carried out at the correct rate and that increases in exercise intensity are not applied too soon. Adaptations in response to one level of overload must occur before the level of overload is increased.

Reversibility: If the tissues are not worked for a period of time they will revert towards their pre-trained state. Adaptations will diminish and fitness and strength gains will be lost.

Specificity: Specific adaptations will occur in the tissues according to the particular type of overload applied (the type of training regularly performed). Different adaptations will occur according to whether aerobic or anaerobic training is predominant. This dictates that specific training has to be performed for specific sports or events.

Running brings about adaptations in the muscular, cardiovascular, respiratory and nervous systems. However, overload must be applied in progressive stages to allow beneficial adaptations to occur and adaptations will only occur if adequate rest is afforded between training sessions.

During training, the physical stresses imposed on the tissues of the body actually cause microscopic damage (micro-trauma) to those tissues. It is during rest periods that the damaged tissues heal, but they heal microscopically stronger than before training. This is known as **over-compensation**, or **super-compensation**.

> Rest is a vital part of a runner's training programme if benefits are to be gained and the risk of injury reduced.

The Main Causes of Running Injuries

It could be suggested that the main causes of running injuries include any, or a combination of, the following:

Progressing too rapidly: Either too much too soon for a beginner, or an excessive increase in mileage for a more experienced runner.

Inadequate rest: Not enough rest between training runs (beginners and older runners may need a longer rest period to allow tissues to recover and adapt); a badly planned training programme which does not incorporate rest days or an alternative activity; inadequate rest after a tough race or marathon; an addiction to running and/or obsession at any level of experience where a person feels guilty if he/she does not run on a particular day, or causes them to run even though they feel particularly tired.

Poor foot biomechanics: The feet are weak and cannot perform properly the function for which they were designed (discussed in more detail in Chapter 7).

Poor running posture: Incorrect spinal alignment and poor core stability puts stress and strain on particular joints, muscles and tissues throughout the body.

Running through an existing 'niggle': A slight pain experienced either during or after a run should be treated, in most cases, with ice and a short rest. Pain is nature's way of informing you that something is wrong, or that something could go very wrong.

Rate of Progression

Complete Beginner

All beginners are not the same. Individual fitness levels can vary considerably. A so-called 'beginner' may have inherited natural ability, whereas another may be totally unfit and will require much longer to reach a certain level and with a slower progression rate. Some people walk the dog on a daily basis, whereas others lead an extremely sedentary life.

Anyone contemplating running for the first time would be advised to start with at least two weeks of regular walking: three half-hour brisk ('power') walks per week with rest days in between. The important thing early on is to be gentle with your body.

After a couple of weeks, progress to three sessions of walking interspersed with short jogging sections; or two walk/jog sessions and one half-hour power walk per week for a further two weeks.

Warming up is important. Start with three or four minutes of power walking as a warm-up for the jog/walk sessions; then complete about six repetitions of one to two minutes jogging and one to two minutes walking (it may be difficult to look at a watch for timing, especially in the dark, so use marker points such as lamp posts); an overall session of about twenty to thirty minutes, finishing with two minutes' brisk walking to cool down.

As weeks go by, progressively increase the length of the jogging sections with adequate recovery walks between. The overall session may be extended to thirty to forty minutes. As speed is not important at this stage, there is no need to increase the intensity. Limit any weekly progression rate to no more than 10 per cent (although it is not possible to increase by 10 per cent indefinitely).

Eventually you should be able to jog a considerable distance without having to walk, although there is nothing wrong with a couple of short recovery walks during an overall session.

KEY POINTS

- Start very gently by walking.
- Increase intensity and duration progressively (no more than 10 per cent per week).
- Do not get impatient or frustrated.
- Start each jogging session with a short walk to warm up.
- 'Listen' to your body. There will be some initial discomfort and aching, but it should not be painful.
- Do not stop suddenly at the end of a jogging section – end with a walking section to cool down.
- Perform a number of gentle stretches at the end.

Although complete novices may prefer another person to accompany them for companionship, safety or confidence, I would *not* recommend starting your running with a seasoned runner. No matter how accommodating they may try to be, no matter how slow they may feel they are running, it will be too fast for you! Nor might they be prepared, or appreciate the need, to walk for part of the session. It is difficult for an experienced runner to perceive exactly how it feels for someone just starting out. What is very easy for the conditioned runner can be very hard for an unfit, complete beginner. It may be better to persuade a like-minded friend to take up the running challenge and progress together according to the advice above.

Shall I Race?

Not everybody has the desire to race and many are happy to run solely for health-related fitness.

Should the challenge of an organized event inspire you, it may be possible as a complete beginner to prepare for a 5-kilometre race in about eight to ten weeks, providing you start and progress correctly, though not everyone will be able to complete 5 kilometres of continuous running after eight weeks. A lot may depend on a person's age, level of previous activity, or genetic make-up. Some people will require a considerably longer period to achieve the ability to jog most, or all, of a 5k race.

For many people, their first 5k 'race' might be the Cancer Research 'Race For Life'. In such an event it is not necessary to actually run the whole distance, and it is not necessarily a race for everyone. It is a charity event, raising money for a very worthwhile cause which gives people a purpose, motivation, great enjoyment and a sense of achievement on completion. Some people will walk the whole distance, others will walk and jog, but many will try to run the whole way.

A recent development in the UK has been the advent of 'Park Races', where you turn up on a Saturday morning at your local park and run a timed 5k along with others and you can use your times to assess improvement (or otherwise).

I would consider it very foolhardy to actually sign up for a 10-kilometre race or half-marathon with absolutely no running experience. This does happen – people see publicity for one of the 'Great' 10k races (e.g. The Great Manchester 10k) and may be persuaded by work colleagues to enter for charity or for a challenge. They may see television coverage of The Great North Run or London Marathon. It looks so easy, but they have no perception of what is actually involved in running, jogging or even jogging/walking 10 kilometres (6.1 miles) or 20 kilometres (13.2 miles). The soul may be willing, but the body is weak. It is much better to develop a level of running fitness and aim for a 5k race and then build up over time to a longer race.

Preparing for a Marathon

I do not intend to offer any sort of marathon training programme, only to discuss some points of guidance to help reduce the risk of injury (which is not guaranteed). Many marathon training schedules exist in books, magazines and on the internet. Some propose going from complete beginner to completing a marathon in sixteen or twenty-four weeks. That might be possible, but it might also be unrealistic for some people. Marathon training should not be contemplated unless you can comfortably run continuously for considerably more than thirty minutes.

A marathon of 26 miles 385 yards (42.195 kilometres) is a long way! It is not something that should be attempted on a whim. I would suggest that if a non-runner decides to aim to complete a marathon he or she should allow a full twelve months to prepare. Although many

people have entered as complete beginners and prepared for a marathon in about twelve months, it would be much safer to develop a considerable level of running fitness and experience before taking the challenge and starting to prepare.

Once established as regular and competent runners, they could complete a number of 10-kilometre races, progress gradually to half-marathon and then allow about six months to prepare for the full marathon. Increases in mileage should be progressive and achievable. Do not suddenly increase your weekly mileage too rapidly.

Physiologically, long runs are the key to marathon training, but in addition to the physiological adaptations that they elicit, other factors are developed. It is important to learn how to keep a constant pace. Successful marathon racing and injury-free training involves maintaining a pace which can be handled throughout. Do not start off too fast.

If your aim is simply to complete the marathon, then regular, steady runs and long, slow distance (LSD) runs will be the mainstay of your training. Those wishing to develop a faster pace may include some interval running or threshold running mid-week. It is important to follow a hard day with a rest day.

Build up your mileage progressively, *no more than 10 per cent per week.* Working life and family commitments vary and it is difficult to suggest on what days of the week to run. However, three comparatively short/moderate distances (between four and eight miles, depending on fitness level) could be run during the week and a longer run at the weekend. The long run will increase progressively week by week (approximately 10 per cent per week) so that by three weeks prior to marathon race day you complete a twenty-mile weekend long run.

The next two weeks should involve tapering and recovery, while maintaining a high carbohydrate diet (which you should have done throughout your training, see Chapter 10).

Rest is absolutely vital, especially after the long run. There may be three rest days per week to allow the body to recover and the tissues to adapt and strengthen.

Should any painful 'niggles' be experienced during marathon training, rest and treat with ice.

Be Prepared for All Types of Weather

Heat, humidity, cold, snow, rain and wind chill can all have a debilitating effect on the body and can increase the risk of (a) typical running injuries to soft tissue and joints, or (b) temperature-related trauma (over-heating, heat stroke, dehydration on the one hand; hypothermia or chilblains on the other).

Core body temperature is 37°C. 'Core' refers to the internal organs and it is vital that this temperature is maintained. The body is remarkable at maintaining correct core temperature under a variety of climatic conditions, but exposure to cold, or exercising in heat and humidity, can overwhelm the body's control systems. Appropriate clothing should be worn according to the climate and weather conditions.

Heat

Severe heat injury may be fairly uncommon in Great Britain, although an occasional hot summer day can present conditions that greatly tax the unconditioned or unacclimatized body and physical stress due to heat can occur. Elite European athletes preparing for races in hot countries or the tropics may spend up to two weeks in hot conditions to acclimatize.

Degrees of Heat Injury

Heat cramps – cramps in the stomach, arms and leg muscles; may be caused by a lack of mineral salts and fluid, through heavy sweating, dehydration, or by lack of conditioning.

Heat syncope – fatigue, weakness, light-headedness and possibly fainting; caused by heavy sweating, dehydration and loss of mineral salts and fluid.

Heat exhaustion – body temperature rises to 40°C. Symptoms include severe thirst, lack of perspiration, vomiting, headaches, weakness, muscle cramps. This condition is serious and must be treated carefully.

Heat stroke – a medical emergency; if not treated properly can result in death due to organ failure. Body temperature rises above 40°C and the body cannot cool itself.

Although trauma from heat can occur during an event (or training run), often it is *at the end* of the activity that the effects can manifest.

Heat syncope can occur at the end of a race or training run. The sudden cessation of movement will reduce air flow across the skin surface and reduce an amount of heat loss by convection. Vasodilatation (widening of blood vessels) increases near the skin surface and central blood volume reduces. Because of the reduction in movement, venous return (blood returning to the heart from the muscles and other organs) is no longer assisted by muscular action. Blood pools in the lower limbs and skin and the resulting hypotension (low blood pressure) can result in collapse. In hot conditions it is even more important not to stop suddenly.

I competed in the Triathlon World Championships in Cancun, Mexico, in 1995 as a member of the Great Britain Masters' Team.

Conditions were sunny with an air temperature of 37°C (90°F) and humidity of about 90 per cent – hardly ideal conditions for racing! It was vital to drink immediately after the swim and then regularly on the bike and running sections. It was also necessary to regularly pour water over my head and, with a very high rate of sweating, my feet were 'sloshing' in my shoes. The medics were very busy throughout the course, especially on the run section and after the finish. I finished in good form, but having crossed the finishing line and then stopping (not abruptly), the heat felt absolutely oppressive. While running we generate a 'breeze' as we move against the air. This can provide some degree of cooling. However, when we stop, that 'breeze' has gone and on that occasion it felt as if a fire had been lit under my feet and the heat rose upwards.

The organizers had provided a water spray tent – a shaded canopy with a framework of pipes with small holes and a constant shower of cool water. This was extremely welcome and helped considerably with my cooling down and recovery, though many were still overcome by heat and the medics had their work cut out.

Cold

The risk of a runner developing some degree of hypothermia is a definite possibility in Great Britain and other European countries, especially during winter, or for those who run on the fells (hill and mountain running). Organizers of fell races usually insist that full waterproof cover is carried along with a map, compass and whistle (mandatory for medium and long Category A races), and may include hat and gloves (Fell Running Association [FRA] rules). The risk increases considerably if it is raining and/or windy. Wet clothing can dramatically increase body heat loss. Wind chill has the effect of the temperature feeling much less than it actually is, increasing body heat loss rapidly from exposed skin.

Injury Due to Cold

Hypothermia is the reduction in body temperature from 37°C to about 35°C.

1. **Mild** – shivering, painful/white fingers.

2. **Moderate** – more violent shivering, reduction in muscle co-ordination, some confusion.

3. **Severe** – very confused, irrational behaviour, slurred speech, very poor muscle co-ordination, decreased heart rate and low blood pressure; can result in organ failure and death; a medical emergency.

As with heat-related trauma, people can suffer during an event, but hypothermia can occur after the finish.

The Greater Manchester Marathon at the end of April 2012 took place in horrendously cold and wet conditions. Many runners suffered en route, but on completion of the race, finishers, already cold, had to queue in wet clothing to try to find their bags containing dry clothing. It was at this stage that many cases of hypothermia occurred and the medical staff were overwhelmed.

The 2013 Wilmslow Half Marathon in Cheshire took place on 24 March during an extremely cold spell – the coldest March for years, with temperatures of 0°C to 2°C and an icy easterly wind producing a severe wind chill. Fortunately, many runners were sensible and dressed appropriately for the conditions and the race organizers had purchased 4,000 space blankets to reduce the risk of hypothermia. Ironically, the previous year's race in March 2012 had taken place in unseasonably hot conditions and overheating was the main problem for runners.

Clothing and Other Considerations for Different Weather Conditions

Hot and humid – Not ideal running conditions; carry a running-designed drink bottle and drink little and often; wear lightweight, wicking materials (cotton is not suitable as it soaks up sweat, becomes heavy and can cause chafing in delicate places) or a running vest. Good quality wicking socks can help to protect from the formation of blisters.

In hot and humid conditions, where the atmosphere is already heavily laden with moisture, evaporation of sweat does not occur readily and the body can overheat. When running, a person will continue to sweat heavily and a vast amount of fluid can be lost from the body by sweating. This fluid will have little cooling effect because it is not evaporating. It is therefore vital to avoid dehydration and to consume regular amounts of water. (See also 'Water/Fluid Intake', Chapter 10.)

Hot, dry and sunny – Worth investing in lightweight, wicking clothing that has sun protection (SPF) qualities. A peaked cap and sunglasses will help to protect your eyes. Use a high SPF (sun protection factor) sport-specific sun lotion on exposed skin to protect against sunburn and the possible development of skin cancer. (See also 'Water/Fluid Intake', Chapter 10.)

Warm and raining – It can be pleasant to run in the rain when the weather is warm; the rain can be quite refreshing. Wicking clothing is recommended that will not soak up the water. Depending on the temperature, shorts and a lightweight shirt or vest can be worn with comfort. If slightly cooler, a lightweight showerproof jacket could be worn (it can be removed and tied round the waist if you become too warm). Again, good wicking socks can protect against blisters.

Cold, frosty, snow and ice – Some people have the idea that running will make us warm and don T-shirt and shorts in the middle of winter; this is asking for trouble. Although heat is generated in the body while running, in cold conditions a considerable amount of heat can be lost, sometimes more than can be generated. Wear a number of layers: a breathable long-sleeved base, another layer on top, preferably breathable and wicking, and a jacket on top. A lot of heat can be lost from the head and so a hat is essential, along with gloves.

Compacted snow can be slippery and particularly dangerous. If such conditions prevail, it is safer not to run. During frosty weather, ice may not always be obvious or visible. Be vigilant for the possibility of icy patches – avoid them, or be prepared to walk over them (better to spend a few seconds walking than a few weeks recovering after a fall).

Cold and windy – Again, dress in layers, including a hat and gloves. Wind chill can cause considerable body heat loss. A showerproof or windproof jacket is recommended.

Cold and raining or sleeting – Cold rain presents very different conditions from warm rain. Cold in itself is a hazard and so layers of clothing are recommended: a wicking base layer, a middle layer and, because of the rain, a waterproof jacket. Do not wear loose-fitting tracksuit bottoms or leggings. They will soak up water, become heavy and flap about. Running-specific, close-fitting leggings/tights are recommended. A hat and gloves are necessary items. After the run do not linger outside; get out of wet clothing and into dry clothes as soon as possible.

Cold, raining or sleeting and windy – Very unpleasant conditions in which to run.

It may be worth having second thoughts and staying indoors. However, if you must run, then dress as described above for cold and rain and include a hat and gloves. Alternatively for health club members, it may be a day for a treadmill session.

Dark nights – See and be seen; concentrate and watch out for pavement hazards (street furniture, raised/cracked paving stones, kerb edges, broken drain covers, etc.). Wear clothing with high visibility reflective panels or strips, or a reflective yellow bib. Run in well-lit areas. Women, ignore and avoid any advances from strangers. Run with a companion.

Some runners choose to listen to music through ear pieces as they run. Though it may be pleasant for them, it is not advisable. They will be less aware of their surroundings.

Fig. 1.2 High visibility reflective strips.

They would not be able to hear traffic, or the bell of a cyclist who may be approaching from behind. It is much better to concentrate, both through sight and sound, on the running environment and to observe and recognize potential hazards.

Running and the Immune System

The immune system is the body's defence against infection. Running may boost the immune system, especially if combined with a good, healthy diet which provides adequate energy along with all essential vitamins and minerals. Running elicits an improvement in all systems of the body and provides the opportunity to breathe fresh air.

Fig. 1.1 Clothing for winter running.

However, an excess of running can suppress the immune system. Adequate rest is essential to allow all the systems of the body to recover and adapt to training. Enthusiasm is good, but obsession is bad. Over-training can result not only in periods of tiredness, but can also lead to chronic fatigue. In turn, this can make the body susceptible to viral infections, or reduce the ability of the immune system to fight off what might start as a minor infection such as a common cold.

Running with a Cold

Should we run with a cold? Whether a novice or experienced runner, caution is advised. If symptoms are not severe and only in the head (runny nose, mild headache) running may be safe, but should be short and easy. Possibly getting out in the fresh air may help 'clear your head' to some degree.

If there are symptoms below the neck such as a chesty cough, aches, pains and a general feel of being unwell, then definitely *do not run*. This is probably a more serious viral infection and the body needs rest for the immune system to fight it. It is important not to run if your temperature is raised above the normal 37°C.

Running with certain viral infections can lead to a more serious condition such as myocarditis, where the virus attacks the heart muscle and may result in death.

CHAPTER 2

WARM-UP AND COOL-DOWN

A correctly performed and appropriate warm-up is essential before any form of physical activity and running is no exception. Likewise, a cool-down at the end of the activity is equally important.

The warm-up prepares the body for the intensity of the exercise to follow, and the cool-down helps the systems of the body recover gradually towards their resting state.

Warm-up

Correct warm-up before running is absolutely vital. It gradually prepares both body and mind for the activity to follow. A variety of physiological changes occur during the warm-up which prepare the body to cope with the physical exertion to follow, enhance the performance, and reduce the risk of injury. Such physiological changes are brought about by low intensity movements and include:

- A gradual increase in heart rate.
- A gradual increase in respiration.
- Redistribution of blood to the working muscles.
- An increase in the supply of oxygen and nutrients to the working muscles.
- An increase in temperature of the working muscles.
- An increase in suppleness of the muscles.
- An increase in the flow of adrenaline.
- Aerobic re-synthesis of ATP (adenosine triphosphate) – the true fuel for muscle contraction – is brought about for prolonged muscle contraction (the aerobic energy system is activated).

A general warm-up should involve low intensity activity to loosen and lubricate those joints to be used and progressively increase heart rate and respiration.

The intensity of the warm-up should be very low to start with, but can increase progressively in intensity throughout its duration. The level of intensity at which it peaks, and the length of the warm-up, will depend on (a) the proposed session to follow (steady health related jog, athletic competition, etc.), and (b) the ability of the performer.

Warm-up before running may simply involve walking at a very low intensity and progressively increasing towards gentle jogging.

I have made no mention yet of static stretching as part of the warm-up, but will discuss the topic now as recent controversy has caused me to consider and assess its value (McHugh and Cosgrave, 2010). It is not advisable to perform static stretches as a warm-up or as the initial part of the warm-up when the muscles are cold. It is not recommended that cold muscles are stretched. Stretching on cold, unprepared muscles is not very effective and in some cases can be quite dangerous (Norris, 2008).

A number of studies now challenge the value of including static stretching as part of a warm-up and its proposed role in injury prevention.

Bromley (1998) debated the value of stretching as part of the warm-up, suggesting it may provide limited benefit. He spoke of the thixotrophic property (stiffness) of muscle at rest and that it is inherently resistant to changes in length. Bonds form between the actin and myosin protein filaments (which are what make up muscles), making the muscle appear comparatively stiff. Gentle movement brings about molecular changes and an increase in temperature in the muscle, making it more ready to change its length. He argued that the general increase in muscle temperature with the molecular changes elicited by low intensity warm-up movements is sufficient to have a stretching effect on the muscle. There is no evidence to suggest that stretching as part of a warm-up has any benefit at all.

I have also heard it argued that the neurological response with static stretching is different to that of dynamic muscle lengthening during exercise movements. Movement and elevation in temperature bring about molecular changes in the muscle tissue making it more supple, with a consequent influence on the joint.

There is increasing debate amongst knowledgeable and well-qualified exercise professionals concerning the value of static stretching as part of the warm-up. It may be that the gentle, progressive movements involved in the warm-up, and the molecular changes and rise in temperature they elicit, are adequate preparation for the more vigorous activity to follow, but some authors do advise stretching as part of the warm-up (Woods et al., 2007; Burfoot, 2009; Jones, 2010; Kay and Blazevich, 2012).

A number of newspaper articles have denounced stretching as 'a waste of time'. Understandably, members of the public have become confused, interpreting the message that stretching per se is a waste of time. Most of the controversy regarding stretching

has resulted from studies which concluded stretching before an activity was ineffective as far as injury prevention was concerned. In the studies, no significant difference in injury rate was found between those who stretched before training or competition and those who did not stretch as part of their warm-up (Pope et al., 2000; Thacker et al., 2004).

However, that does not mean that stretching has no value per se. Regular static (long-held/non-bouncing) stretching, particularly after an activity, increases muscle suppleness and therefore joint flexibility. Increased flexibility should have a beneficial influence on athletic performance and should help to reduce the risk of injury (Woods et al., 2007: Norris, 2008). Stretching should form a vital part of any training programme.

In addition, studies have focused on the influence of pre-stretching (as part of a warm-up) on injury prevention, not its influence on performance during competition. Whether or not pre-stretching improves performance in the event to follow is debatable. Curry et al. (2009) reported that dynamic stretching in the warm-up has a greater applicability to enhance performance on power outcomes compared to static stretching. Physiological benefit may be debatable, but if there is a psychological benefit, then it is perhaps of value. If a person feels psychologically more prepared for his or her event as a result of pre-stretching, then it may enhance the performance to follow and in that respect may be worthwhile

Anderson and Anderson (2010) suggested gentle stretches may be performed after an initial warm-up and then a second warm-up performed. They did emphasize the importance of stretching as part of the cool-down.

Baird (2006) does not mention stretching during warm-up, but does stress the importance of stretching as part of the cool-down.

Cool-down

Cool-down is absolutely essential at the end of a running session. It is potentially dangerous to stop suddenly at the end of a vigorous activity and an appropriate cool-down should always be performed. The cool-down is a continuation of activity at a reduced intensity.

Towards the end of the cool-down a series of stretches should be performed while the muscles are still very warm. Stretches may be held for twenty to thirty seconds and can be particularly effective for the maintenance and development of flexibility.

The cool-down allows the systems of the body to return gradually towards their resting state without too much abrupt change. Heart rate remains elevated, but gradually decreases, assisting in the removal of waste

A CAUTIONARY TALE

In 1977, an American journalist called Jim Fixx wrote the best-selling *The Complete Book of Running*, which inspired many Americans to run and turned the author into a running legend.

Jim Fixx took up running later in life, but was so inspired by the many health benefits he regularly ran sixty to seventy miles per week. He wrote more books and articles extolling the benefits of running and became a 'hero' to the ever-increasing running fraternity. Then on 20 July 1984 Jim Fixx died of a heart attack during a training run and the running world was thrown into confusion and disbelief.

It should be noted, however, that before he took up running, Jim Fixx had led a stressful life as a journalist, eating, drinking and smoking to excess. He had been sedentary and overweight. He had a father who had died of a heart attack at forty-three, which, incidentally, might have been his fate years earlier were it not for his running. He had also suffered previous minor heart attacks, about which he may or may not have been aware. It should also remembered that he was not an advocate of healthy eating and thought that running on its own was enough to promote health.

After his death, a post mortem examination showed scar tissue on his heart muscle from previous heart attacks and his coronary arteries, which supply oxygenated blood to the heart muscle itself, were considerably narrowed by fatty deposits. On that final run in 1984 his heart had reached a state where it could not cope. It appears he cut short his run, possibly because he felt something was wrong. He stopped suddenly and then passed out.

And here is the main point of this story: because he stopped suddenly (definitely not recommended), his heart rate probably rose to a very high level and went into ventricular fibrillation (very rapid and ineffectual fluttering). He collapsed to his knees, but with his upper body propped in an almost upright position against a bank. In this position his blood pressure would have been comparatively low and the blood could not flow upwards towards his heart.

It is possible that, with his enlarged heart (not athletically enlarged, but pathologically enlarged) and clogged coronary arteries, the heart attack was severe and may have killed him before he collapsed. However, the fact that he remained motionless in an upright position prohibited even the remotest chance of survival.

This illustrates the importance of never stopping suddenly during physical activity and how important the cool-down really is.

products from the muscles. Continuing movement prevents blood pooling in the lower limbs, maintaining circulation and the return of venous blood to the heart. Blood pressure is maintained and, therefore, the supply of arterial blood to the brain, thus reducing the possibility of light-headedness and fainting. Also blood supply to the heart is maintained.

Maintenance of circulation and the preservation of blood pressure go hand-in-hand.

During vigorous activity adrenaline and related hormones are secreted into the blood stream to stimulate muscle contraction and heart rate. If the activity ceases suddenly, blood pressure can fall dramatically. Adrenaline stimulates the heart to beat faster but inefficiently in an attempt to increase blood pressure. However, it may not be able to achieve this and blood supply to the tissues of the heart itself may be inadequate. Greater stress is then placed on the heart muscle (Cooper, 1980, 1986).

CHAPTER 3

STRETCHING, SUPPLENESS AND FLEXIBILITY

Suppleness is a condition of the muscles whereby they have the ability to relax and lengthen to their full potential. **Flexibility** refers to the range of movement in joints. Suppleness of the muscles should therefore allow good flexibility of the joints (Smith, 1994; Pearson, 1998).

The development and maintenance of suppleness and flexibility is important for runners and may help to reduce the risk of both traumatic and overuse injuries.

Movement encourages the secretion of synovial fluid into the joint. Movable joints are surrounded and supported by a joint capsule of strong ligamentous tissue. Within that joint capsule is a synovial membrane (freely movable joints are also known as synovial joints). The synovial membrane secretes synovial fluid into the joint to lubricate and nourish the articular surfaces of the joint. Movement is the stimulus for the secretion of synovial fluid.

Regular movement also affects the muscles in many positive ways, which in turn influence the joints. For every movement that occurs, muscles are not only shortening to cause that movement, but other muscles lengthen to control the movement. This lengthening of the antagonist muscle has a 'stretching' effect on the muscle and helps to develop and maintain its lengthening potential.

Muscles can become shortened and tight because of repetitive part-range movements. Synovial joints have a potential full range of movement; with a typical hinge joint that full range is from fully extended (straightened) to fully flexed (bent). Running involves movement of joints through only a part of their range. This can have a shortening effect on the muscle, which will in turn restrict flexibility of the joint.

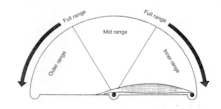

Fig. 3.1   A typical hinge joint illustrating the potential full range of movement from fully extended to fully flexed, and the different sections of that full range (the diagram resembles an arm from the shoulder [bottom right], biceps muscle [shaded], elbow [bottom centre], forearm and hand [bottom left]).

Mobilizing the joints as part of the warm-up helps to lubricate the joint by the secretion of synovial fluid, but also warms up and loosens the related muscles. As the muscles become less stiff during movement, then the short-term flexibility of the joint increases.

Control is important, and control should

be maintained with all movements. Fast, jerky, ballistic (bouncy) movements of joints can be potentially harmful. Joints should not be moved forcefully and ballistically to the end of their normal range. This can cause excessive stress to the specific ligaments and the joint capsule, resulting in possible micro-damage and inflammation. Although short-term flexibility may be achieved this is unlikely to be sustained.

Although flexibility can be restricted by injury, disease or deterioration of a joint, in a healthy joint the main restriction to flexibility will be the muscles that control that joint. The lengthening potential of the antagonist muscle is the main limiting factor in joint flexibility.

Basic Principles of Stretching

We stretch to increase the lengthening potential of the muscles, which in turn allows good flexibility at the joints. Stretching, and the flexibility it affords, is a vital part of any training programme, whether for health-related benefits or for sporting performance. There are three types of stretching; **ballistic**, **static** and **dynamic** (also known as range of movement [ROM]).

Ballistic stretching involves lengthening a muscle to its comfortable achievable length and then bouncing. This type of stretching is not generally recommended as it involves a number of potential dangers.

Ballistic stretching can invoke a powerful stretch reflex in the muscle which results in contractile tension, the opposite of what we are trying to achieve. With the fibres attempting to contract, and gravity or momentum forcing them to lengthen, there is the potential for muscle fibre damage.

The collagen connective tissue in the muscle is comparatively inelastic. When warm it can become pliable, but takes time to elongate. During fast ballistic bouncing of the muscle there is no time for the connective tissue to elongate.

Bouncing can cause microscopic tears in the muscle fibres and connective tissue. The tears then heal with scar tissue, which reduces the muscle's elasticity and may subsequently limit flexibility (Pullig-Schaltz, 1994).

Static stretching is much safer and more effective. Static stretching involves slowly lengthening the muscle to its full achievable length and then holding that stretch position.

This not only develops the ability for the muscle fibres to elongate effectively, but, if performed when the muscles are warm (as all stretching should be), allows time for the connective tissue in the muscle to microscopically elongate.

It is the connective tissue in the muscle that we are really trying to influence by stretching. The muscle's connective tissue consists mainly of collagen fibres. Collagen is relatively inelastic and cannot change its length or return quickly. However, when very warm it can become 'plastic' and pliable (it can elongate slowly but does not return to its original length quickly).

It is very important, therefore, that we stretch muscles when they are very warm and have achieved a temperature whereby the connective tissue has become pliable (Bromley, 1998; Pearson, 1998; Norris, 1994, 2008). Stretching is therefore very beneficial immediately at the end of a run.

Static stretching can be active (the stretch is carried out by the performer alone) or passive (the stretch position is achieved with the assistance of another person or another force).

Dynamic stretching involves moving a joint through its range using controlled movements (not bouncing), thereby taking the muscles in and out of a lengthened position. It can be performed as part of a warm-up prior to training or competition. Static stretching therefore is not necessarily performed as part of the warm-up, but should be performed as part of a cool-down for both maintenance and the development of suppleness and flexibility.

Maintenance stretches are sometimes referred to as short-held stretches and are held for seven to ten seconds (Smith, 1994; Lycholat, 1995; Pearson, 1998).

Developmental stretches are sometimes referred to as long-held stretches. They should be performed at the end of a run when the muscles are very warm and positions are held for approximately twenty to thirty seconds (Smith, 1994; Lycholat, 1995; Pearson, 1998).

Stretch positions should be achieved whereby a degree of stretch tension is felt, but not to the extent of pain (American College of Sports Medicine [ACSM], 1986). The position is then held relatively comfortably. If an excess of tension develops then the position should be relaxed and the stretch reduced.

Remember that muscles are not like elastic which can literally be stretched by lengthening and then will relax back to a shortened state. Muscles work by contracting and relax by lengthening. If the lengthening is slow and not against gravity, then the stretch reflex can be de-sensitized and the muscle will truly relax rather than attempting an eccentric (lengthening) contraction. True relaxation is what we are aiming for during stretching exercises.

Stretch Reflex

There exists in the muscle sensory structures known as muscle spindles. These proprio-

ceptors are positioned alongside the muscle fibres and recognize even the most microscopic lengthening of the fibres.

When muscle fibres lengthen and the muscle spindle detects the lengthening, the information is transmitted via a sensory nerve to the central nervous system. The information is processed in the spinal cord and a message returns via a motor nerve telling the muscle fibres to contract.

This is a reflex action and occurs (as far as we can consciously perceive) instantly. Reflex actions occur so quickly because the information is processed in the grey matter of the spinal cord and does not have to be sent further up to 'head office' (the main brain), so to speak.

It should be obvious that the stretch reflex is the basis of muscle tone whereby muscles can develop tension instantly and in proportion to the resistance or force applied. Simply put, if a muscle is lengthened, usually by the force of gravity, it will resist that lengthening as its fibres attempt to contract and develop tension.

It should also be obvious that ballistic stretching causes a very quick and forceful lengthening of the fibres and consequently the stretch reflex causes tension in the muscle.

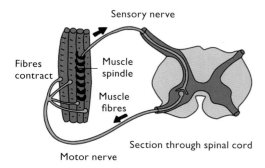

Fig. 3.2 Diagrammatic representation of the stretch reflex.

Inverse Stretch Reflex

Inverse stretch reflex is another proprioceptive mechanism that can cause the muscle to relax if extremes of tension develop – for example, if a very heavy weight is suddenly placed in the hands and we immediately drop it. It is not a conscious decision to drop the weight, but a reflex action that occurs a fraction of a second before we make the conscious decision.

There exists in the muscle-tendon junction a sensory structure known as the Golgi Tendon Organ (GTO). The GTO recognizes high tension in the muscle and sends a message via a sensory nerve to the central nervous system. Again the information is processed in the spinal cord and a message returns via a motor nerve telling the muscle fibres to relax.

The inverse stretch reflex is a safety device intended to prevent damage to the muscle, which might occur if excesses of tension were allowed to develop. Authorities appear to differ in opinion as to what invokes the inverse stretch reflex. Some suggest the GTO is stimulated by stretch tension, and that holding a stretch position for longer than about seven seconds causes the muscle to relax.

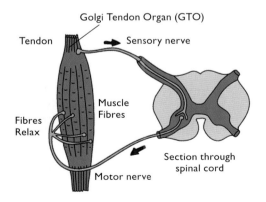

Fig. 3.3   Diagrammatic representation of the inverse stretch reflex.

Others suggest it only responds to contractile tension.

Proprioceptive Neuromuscular Facilitation (PNF) Stretching

We can make use of the inverse stretch reflex to increase the effect of developmental stretching. PNF stretching involves positioning a limb so that a static stretch is achieved in the selected muscle. The stretch position is held for a few seconds and then the performer pushes back against a resistance (may be a resistance applied by a partner [passive]). This causes high contractile isometric tension to develop in the muscle which has previously been stretched. The isometric contraction is held for about four seconds and then the performer relaxes again. The stretch position can now be resumed and the stretch increased because the inverse stretch reflex has caused the muscle fibres to relax even further.

PNF stretching is often performed passively with assistance from a partner, who moves the limb to achieve a position whereby the target muscle is lengthened. The partner then applies the resistance against which that muscle contracts. Then the partner assists with the subsequent stretch position, which should increase its range.

Whenever passive stretching is performed, either as static stretching or as PNF stretching, the partner must act in a very responsible manner otherwise injury could occur. The partner must avoid any fast or sudden movements and must communicate with the performer to establish when stretch limits are comfortably achieved. Do not attempt to take the stretch any further than that which the performer has indicated. When terminating the stretch position, do not allow a limb to drop suddenly with gravity. In a controlled manner, slowly lower the limb to the starting position.

Guidelines for Safe and Effective Stretching

- Stretch warm muscles.
- Perform static or dynamic stretches in preference to ballistic stretches.
- Hold stretch positions for a minimum of seven seconds, but preferably for approximately twenty to thirty seconds.
- Achieve stretch positions whereby the muscle is not 'holding back' against gravity and can therefore relax.
- Stretch at the end of every run.
- Do not over-stretch; keep within the limits of pain.

Suggested Stretches for Runners

All the stretches increase the suppleness of the stretched muscle and may reduce muscle strain.

Calf Stretches

There are two major muscles which make up those referred to as the calf muscles: gastrocnemius and soleus. Both insert to the back of the heel bone via the Achilles tendon, but have separate origins. Gastrocnemius splits into two heads, crosses the back of the knee joint and attaches to the posterior medial and posterior lateral aspect of the femur (thigh bone). Soleus attaches to the posterior surface of the tibia (shin bone) and does not cross the knee joint. When stretching the calf muscles, this anatomical knowledge is important and we must remember to stretch in such a way as to emphasize each muscle separately.

Gastrocnemius Stretch

Stand facing a wall and rest both hands on the wall. Place one foot backwards and slowly lower the heel of that foot to the floor. Keep

Fig. 3.4   Free-standing gastrocnemius stretch.

the back knee fully extended so that the leg is straight. Because gastrocnemius crosses and attaches above the knee joint, gastrocnemius is therefore emphasized. Hold that position for about twenty seconds and then repeat with the other leg. To increase the stretch move the back foot further back, but make sure the heel goes comfortably to the floor. Alternatively perform a free-standing gastrocnemius stretch.

Soleus Stretch

Stand facing a wall, about half a metre away. Dorsi-flex (bend foot and toes towards head) one foot and rest the toes of that foot against the wall with the heel on the floor. The knee of that leg will be slightly flexed.

Fig. 3.5   Gastrocnemius stretch against a wall.

Increase that knee flexion further and slowly move that knee towards the wall. This will increase the stretch in the calf region. Because soleus attaches below the knee joint and the knee is flexed, soleus is therefore emphasized. Hold that position for about twenty seconds and then repeat with the other leg. Alternatively perform a free-standing soleus stretch.

Quadriceps Stretches

The quadriceps form the group of four muscles at the front of the thigh and include vastus lateralis, vastus intermedius, vastus medialis and rectus femoris. The three vasti muscles have their origin attached to the femur, whereas rectus femoris crosses the hip joint. The vasti muscles are directly responsible for extending the knee joint. Rectus femoris, though assisting with knee extension, also assists with hip flexion.

Standing Quadriceps Stretch

Stand on one foot, either in balance or using a support to hold on to. Flex the knee of the

Fig. 3.6   Free-standing soleus stretch.

Fig. 3.7 Soleus stretch against a wall.

Figs 3.8 and 3.9 ABOVE AND BELOW: Standing quadriceps stretch.

other leg and take hold of that foot. Slowly pull that foot towards the buttock to fully lengthen the quadriceps at the front of the thigh. Hold for about twenty seconds and then repeat for the other thigh. Make sure the thigh is parallel to the other thigh and pointing downwards.

Prone-lying Quadriceps Stretch

Lie on the floor/mat face down. As with the standing quadriceps stretch, flex one knee. Take hold of that foot and slowly pull the heel towards the buttock to stretch the front of the thigh. Stabilize the spine and push the hip forwards to include rectus femoris.

As one of the quadriceps muscles, rectus femoris, also crosses the hip joint, it is important to push the hip forwards and emphasize this muscle. However, do not push the hip forwards in such a way that the lumbar spine is hyper-extended. Be aware of the spine and try to maintain neutral (straight) alignment. Use the abdominal muscles to stabilize the lumbar spine.

Hamstring Stretches

The hamstrings are the muscles at the back of the thigh and consist of three muscles, semitendinosus, semimembranosus and biceps femoris. All three muscles cross the back of the knee joint to insert into the lateral and medial condyles of the tibia. At the top they share a common origin from the ischium of the pelvis.

Individual Hamstring Stretch, Standing

This is a comparatively safe method of stretching the hamstrings because body weight is supported on one leg alone and we stretch

Fig. 3.10   Prone-lying quadriceps stretch.

To stretch the hamstrings we must achieve full knee extension and hip flexion. However, we need to achieve a position whereby the hamstrings can relax and do not try to hold an eccentric contraction.

the hamstrings of the non-weight-bearing leg. Also placing the hands on the thigh of the slightly-bent weight-bearing leg supports the upper body weight and protects the spine.

Stand with the weight on one leg, the knee of that leg slightly flexed. Straighten out the other leg forwards with the heel resting on the floor. Place the hands on the thigh of the weight-bearing leg and bend forwards from the hip. Feel the stretch in the hamstrings of the straight leg.

Hamstring Stretch Standing with One Leg Supported

Lift one leg so that the heel can rest on a raised object such as a low wall, step bench, weight training bench, chair, etc. Keep the knee extended and lean forwards slowly, flexing from the hip joint. Hold that position for about twenty seconds.

Specific hamstring muscles can be targeted by varying the position of the support/standing leg.

Supine-lying Hamstring Stretch

Lie supine (face up) on the floor or cushioned mat. Have one knee flexed and that foot on the floor. Lift the other leg and grasp that leg with both hands around the knee or calf region. Slowly pull that leg towards the chest and try to keep the knee extended. If you cannot fully extend the knee, do not try to force it. Hold that position for about twenty seconds and then repeat with the other leg. Do not lift the pelvis off the floor.

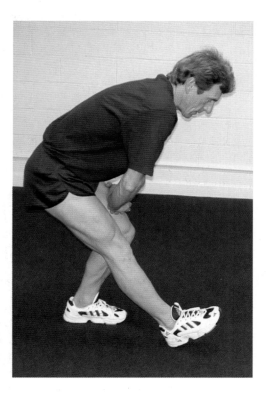

Fig. 3.11 Individual hamstring stretch, standing.

If the standing foot points forwards, the raised and supported leg tends to roll outwards because of lateral rotation of the hip. This emphasizes the stretch on the outer hamstring (biceps femoris). If the standing foot is turned out slightly to the side, the raised and supported leg tends to roll inwards because of medial rotation of the hip joint. This emphasizes the inner hamstrings (semitendinosus and semimembranosus).

Figs 3.12a and 3.12b   Hamstring stretch standing with one leg supported, (a) standing foot pointing forwards emphasizing the outer hamstring muscles, (b) standing foot turned outwards emphasizing the inner hamstring muscle.

Individual Hamstring Stretch Seated on the Floor

Sit on the floor with one leg stretched out, the other leg comfortably placed with the knee flexed and the foot on the floor. Bend forwards from the hip joint to stretch the hamstring on the back of the thigh of the outstretched leg. Hold for about twenty seconds and then repeat with the other leg. Do not force the back into hyper-flexion.

Hamstring Stretch Seated on a Bench

Sit on a bench (e.g. changing room bench or bench in the gym) with one leg outstretched along the bench. Position the other leg by the side of the bench with the foot on the floor. Bend forwards from the hip joint to stretch the hamstrings of the outstretched leg. Hold for about twenty seconds and then repeat with the other leg outstretched. This is a very good stretch to perform in the sauna where it is very warm, seated with one leg

ABOVE: Fig. 3.13   Supine-lying hamstring stretch.

BELOW: Figs 3.14 and 3.15   Individual hamstring stretch on the floor.

Fig. 3.16   No need to touch the toes if you cannot reach.

Figs 3.17a and 3.17b   Hamstring stretch seated on a bench, (a) emphasizing the outer hamstring muscles, (b) emphasizing the inner hamstring muscle.

As with the standing hamstring stretch with one leg supported, the outer or inner hamstrings can be emphasized by positioning the other thigh (a) parallel to the bench (outer), or (b) turned out away from the bench (inner).

Fig. 3.18 Passive (partner-assisted) stretch for the hamstrings.

Communicate with the subject at all times and do not attempt to push further than he/she finds comfortable. Movements should be slow and controlled.

outstretched along the bench and the foot of the other leg resting on a lower bench or floor.

Passive (Partner-assisted) Hamstring Stretch
The subject lies supine on the floor/mat with one knee flexed, foot on the floor, the other leg out straight. The partner kneels by the side and lifts the performer's straight leg. A hand is placed around the heel or back of the subject's lower leg in order to push and the other hand goes just beyond the knee on the thigh to stabilize and maintain an extended knee (do not place the hand directly over the knee cap). Slowly push the straight leg to achieve a well-flexed hip and hold for about twenty seconds. Repeat with the other leg.

Passive PNF Stretch for the Hamstrings
Exactly the same as described above, but hold the stretch for about seven seconds. Then ask the subject to push back for about four seconds against your resistance (thus forcefully contracting the hamstrings and gluteals). The subject then relaxes and the partner pushes the leg slightly further than before, but still within the subject's capability.

The Potential Dangers of Traditional Standing 'Toe-touch' Hamstring Stretches
Some traditional methods of hamstring stretching are now considered to be potentially dangerous and less effective.

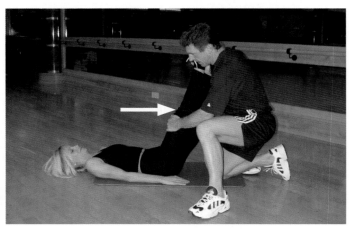

Figs. 3.19a, b and c   Passive PNF stretch for the hamstrings: (a) the initial stretch, (b) the subject pushes back, (c) the hamstrings are stretched further.

Fig. 3.20 Standing 'toe-touch' hamstring stretch – not recommended.

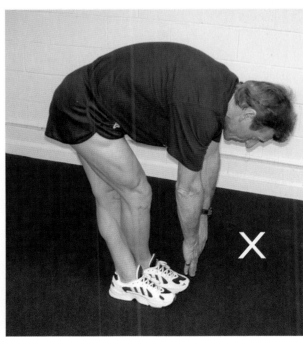

Fig. 3.21 Standing 'toe-touch' hamstring stretch with crossed feet – not recommended.

Standing and bending forwards to reach towards, or touch, the toes is potentially very dangerous for the lumbar spine. Inter-vertebral disc pressure is raised and there is the risk of disc prolapse or herniation. Also the extensor muscles of the spine have difficulty in holding the required eccentric contraction. They may tear or go into spasm. The many tiny ligaments of the spinal joints have to bear the majority of the body weight and there is a risk of ligament damage. This may result in pain.

In this position the hamstring muscles attempt a strong eccentric contraction in order to hold the body against gravity. They are forcefully lengthened because of the position, yet try to contract. This eccentric contraction is not the same as true relaxation and negative tension occurs in the muscles, the opposite of what we actually desire.

Fig. 3.22
Individual knee tuck gluteal stretch (single leg hug).

Fig. 3.23
Individual gluteal stretch supine-lying with one foot crossed over the other knee.

There is the risk of damaging the hamstrings microscopically and in the long term reducing suppleness and flexibility.

The practice of crossing over the feet and then bending forwards is also not recommended. The same theory applies as described above concerning the safety of the spine and the possible long-term effect on the hamstrings. However, now we also have the question of balance and the risk of sudden movements which can cause muscle tears.

Gluteal Stretches

The gluteal muscles consist of gluteus maximus, gluteus medius and gluteus minimus. Gluteus maximus is the main extensor of the hip.

Lie on your back on the floor/mat with the knees flexed and the feet on the floor. Tuck one knee towards the chest and grasp with the hand. Slowly pull that knee further towards the chest, increasing the flexion of the hip. Hold for about twenty seconds and then repeat with the other leg (Fig. 3.22).

Individual Gluteal Stretch Supine-lying with One Foot Crossed over the Other Knee

Lie on your back on the floor/mat with one knee flexed and the foot on the floor. Flex the other knee and rotate the hip to rest that ankle across the knee or thigh on the flexed resting leg. Place the arms around the flexed resting thigh, link the fingers and slowly pull that thigh towards the chest. Feel the stretch in the buttock region of the crossed-over leg. Hold for about twenty seconds and then repeat with the other leg (Fig. 3.23).

Stretches for the Inner Thigh (Adductors)

The adductor muscles consist of gracilis, pectineus, adductor longus, adductor brevis, adductor magnus.

Standing Adductor Stretch

Muscles stretched: All adductor muscles including gracilis which crosses the knee joint medially.

Stand with the legs apart and turn one foot outwards to adopt a lunge position to that side but keep the upper body facing forwards and upright. Rest the hand on the top of the trailing thigh and gently press downwards. The stretch should be felt on the inner aspect of that thigh. Hold this position for about twenty seconds and then repeat for the other leg.

Fig. 3.24   Standing adductor stretch.

People may consider this position is influencing (stretching) the front thigh of the bent lunge leg because they feel tension in that thigh. This tension is in the quadriceps, which are holding an isometric contraction to maintain the stance. The *stretch* is in the adductor muscles of the other thigh.

Seated Adductor Stretch

Sit on the floor with the back either unsupported or against a wall. Flex both knees and bring the soles of the feet together. Grasp the feet with both hands and rest your elbows on the inside of your knees. Slowly press the knees outwards with the elbows. Hold this position for about twenty seconds.

Stretches for the Outer Thigh (Abductors)

Fig. 3.26   Standing abductor stretch.

The abductor muscles consist of gluteus medius and tensor fascia latae.

Fig. 3.25   Seated adductor stretch.

Standing Abductor Stretch

Stand sideways on to a wall about half a metre away. Cross the foot nearest the wall over and behind the other foot. Lean sideways towards the wall. Resting your hand on the wall, take your body weight and control the lean towards the wall. Exaggerate the lean by slowly pushing your hip towards the wall. A stretch should occur in the outer thigh of the leg nearest the wall.

Seated Abductor Stretch

Sit on a mat with legs outstretched. Cross the left foot over the right leg and position that foot on the floor on the outer side of the right knee. Place the left hand on the floor behind and to the left of the body to support the upper body and with the right hand pull the left knee over towards the right. Hold that position for about twenty seconds and repeat for the other side. Maintain an upright and neutral spine throughout.

Hip Flexor Stretch

The major hip flexor muscles include iliacus, which has its origin attachment on the inner aspect of the ilium (part of the pelvic bone), and the psoas major, which has its origin attached to the lumbar and sacral spine. Both muscles insert to one common attachment on the lesser trochanter of the femur. They are often referred to as one muscle, ilio-psoas. Also involved in hip flexion is rectus femoris, one of the quadriceps muscles which crosses the front of the hip joint.

Kneeling Hip Flexor Stretch

Adopt a kneeling position with the front

Fig. 3.27 Seated abductor stretch.

It is important to stretch and lengthen the hip flexor muscles. They can be prone to shortening, which tilts the pelvis forwards from the top and exaggerates the forward curve of the lumbar spine. This postural position (lordosis) is often accompanied by shortened spinal extensors and length-ened abdominals.

lower leg vertical so that the knee does not go beyond the line of the toes. Allow the toe

of the back leg to point backwards. Without arching (hyper-extending) the lower back, push the hip forwards keeping the back knee down on the floor. Feel the stretch in the groin area and top of the thigh of the trailing leg. Hold for about twenty seconds and then repeat with the other leg.

Supine-lying Hip Flexor Stretch

Lie on your back on a high bench or table so that your buttock is supported but your legs trail over the end to hang downwards. Tuck one leg towards your chest and grasp with the hands, slowly pulling further towards

Fig. 3.28   Kneeling hip flexor stretch.

Fig. 3.29   Supine-lying hip flexor stretch.

the chest. Hold this position for about twenty seconds and then repeat, tucking the other leg.

Suggested Post-run Stretches

Immediately at the end of a run, and while the muscles are still warm, a series of stretches should be performed as part of the general cool-down, focusing on the main muscles involved in running. These stretches can be held for about twenty seconds.

1. Calf stretch (gastrocnemius).
2. Calf stretch (soleus).
3. Quadriceps stretch.
4. Hamstring stretch.
5. Adductor stretch.
6. Abductor stretch.
7. Gluteal stretch.
8. Hip flexor stretch.

CHAPTER 4

THE ENERGY SYSTEMS

For runners, a knowledge of aerobic and anaerobic is not complete without a basic understanding of the energy systems. In much the same way as a car engine produces energy by the combustion of petrol with oxygen, energy is produced in the muscle by the metabolism of fuels. However, the body can produce energy both with oxygen (**aerobic metabolism**) and without oxygen (**anaerobic metabolism**).

When producing energy with oxygen, and therefore at low to moderate intensities, the waste products of metabolism are converted ultimately to carbon dioxide and water, which are easily processed and disposed of. Therefore the activity can continue for longer periods of time.

When we work at high intensities, energy is produced without oxygen, and the waste product remains at the lactic acid stage. In the absence of oxygen, lactic acid will accumulate in the muscles and the blood and will eventually prevent muscle contraction. A painful, burning sensation will be felt in the muscles and the activity can only last for a comparatively short period of time.

It is commonly considered that the food we eat is fuel for energy production. In a sense this is true, but to be precise, food provides substances which create the fuel for energy production.

Stored within the muscle is a chemical compound called **adenosine triphosphate (ATP)**. ATP must be present for energy to be produced. However, there is only enough ATP stored in the muscle for about one or two muscular contractions. So there must exist a process by which more ATP is generated immediately so that energy production and muscle contraction can continue. This is where we utilize the three energy systems. The first two are anaerobic, and the third is aerobic.

1. The Creatine Phosphate System (Anaerobic/Alactate)

ATP is broken down to ADP (adenosine diphosphate) to produce energy. Creatine phosphate (CP) combines with ADP to produce more ATP and energy production can continue. However, there is only enough CP stored in the muscle for about ten seconds of energy production.

ATP (broken down to ADP) = energy

ADP + CP (enough CP for approx. 10 seconds)

2. The Glycogen (Lactate) System (Anaerobic)

If the activity is to continue when CP is temporarily exhausted, glycogen is combined with ADP to create more ATP, but now pyruvic acid is produced as a waste product. In the absence of oxygen, the pyruvic acid is converted to lactic acid which can accumulate in the muscles and the blood. At higher intensities energy production can only last for a few minutes before fatigue sets in due to lactic acid build-up.

ATP (broken down to ADP) = energy + pyruvic acid (without oxygen) lactic acid

ADP + glycogen

3. The Aerobic System

If we are working at lower intensities, we may go through the first two stages of energy production, but eventually the muscles take up oxygen and the aerobic system becomes predominant.

Fatty acids and glycogen are combined with the ADP to produce more ATP. This process occurs in the presence of oxygen and now the waste product, pyruvic acid, is converted completely to carbon dioxide and water, which are easily processed and do not accumulate. Therefore the activity can continue for much longer periods of time.

ATP (broken down to ADP) = energy + pyruvic acid (with oxygen) CO_2 + H_2O

ADP + fat + glycogen

Types of Running

The type of running performed will target and improve specific energy pathways. The three energy systems can be specifically trained to be more effective and more efficient.

Long, slow distance running (LSD), in the 60–70 per cent max HR (fat burning) zone, the main-stay of marathon training, targets the aerobic energy system. As well as improving the transport and uptake of oxygen for energy production in the muscle cells, it improves the body's ability to metabolize fat as fuel, therefore conserving valuable glycogen stores in the muscles. Precise aerobic adaptations are discussed in a later chapter.

Interval running and threshold training will influence all energy systems. There will be some focus on the aerobic energy pathways during recovery sections, but also on the anaerobic energy pathways, particularly the glycogen energy system. Interval training can increase the body's ability to tolerate and process lactic acid as well as increasing the rate at which lactic acid accumulates (raise the anaerobic threshold).

Sprint training, working regularly at high intensities to employ the fast-twitch muscle fibres, will focus on the anaerobic energy pathways, both the creatine phosphate and glycogen systems, and will train the body to store more creatine phosphate in the muscles (though there is a limit to how much can be stored).

CHAPTER 5

DETERMINING TRAINING INTENSITIES

Aerobic and Anaerobic Defined and Explained

Running is an aerobic activity. The word **aerobic** means **with oxygen**. The opposite is **anaerobic**, which means **without oxygen**. The word **aerobics** was introduced by the American doctor, Kenneth Cooper, to refer to aerobic conditioning exercise, or the type of exercise which has a conditioning effect on the oxygen transport systems of the body. The oxygen transport systems of the body consist of the cardiovascular system and the respiratory system. As they are so closely related they are sometimes referred to as one combined system, the **cardio-respiratory system**, or the **aerobic system**, and are made up of the heart, lungs and circulatory system.

In Britain the word 'aerobics' has been adopted to refer to the type of teacher-led exercise class carried out to music. Although such a session will consist of a number of different components including warm-up, pre-stretch, cool-down, post-stretch, toning and strengthening, developmental stretch and relaxation, a major component of that session will be devoted to aerobic conditioning, hence the use of the word.

Aerobic conditioning exercise, or aerobic training, involves longer duration rhythmic exercises employing large muscle groups that demand large quantities of oxygen delivered by greater quantities of blood. The blood and oxygen is supplied by the cardio-respiratory system, which consequently has to work harder. According to training principles, the cardio-respiratory system is overloaded, stressed, and eventually adapts to become more effective and more efficient at supplying oxygen.

If we are exercising aerobically we are working at an intensity whereby the cardio-respiratory system can constantly supply enough oxygen to the working muscle cells. With an adequate supply of oxygen, energy is produced in the muscles by the metabolism of carbohydrate and fat. The waste product given off is pyruvic acid. In the presence of oxygen, pyruvic acid is completely broken down to carbon dioxide and water, which is easily removed and eliminated, and so the exercise can continue within that range of intensity.

If we exercise harder we eventually reach an intensity where we are working anaerobically. At a certain higher level of intensity (referred to as anaerobic threshold, which varies from person to person according to their fitness level or state of training) the cardio-respiratory system cannot supply enough oxygen to the working muscle. Therefore the muscle has to produce energy without adequate oxygen. This situation cannot last for very long as now an increased amount of carbohydrate is metabolized without adequate oxygen and the waste product given off is converted to lactic acid, which begins to accumulate in the muscle and in the blood. The accumulation of lactic acid eventually prevents the muscles from contracting and a painful feeling is experienced.

It should be obvious then that aerobic conditioning exercise (or working aerobically) involves working at a lower/moderate intensity. Through such training we develop cardio-respiratory stamina, the ability to maintain the activity for longer periods of time. Changes (adaptations) occur in the lungs, the heart muscle, and the circulatory system, which improve the ability of the systems to transport and supply oxygen. Adaptations also occur in the muscles, improving their ability to work for longer periods of time. These adaptations are discussed in the next chapter.

There are three variables with aerobic conditioning exercise/training, which are often referred to as the FIT variables. F = frequency (how often we exercise); I = intensity (how hard we exercise); T = time (or duration – how long we exercise). They are variables because as our aerobic fitness increases, any one, or all three variables can change; we can train more often, at higher intensities, and for longer periods of time.

A beginner may be advised to train three times per week at low to moderate intensities (comfortable) for fifteen to thirty minutes per session (ACSM, 1986). Experienced competitive athletes may train five or six times per week, or in some cases twice a day, at higher intensities nearer to their anaerobic threshold, and for periods of an hour or more in order to 'fine tune' the cardio-respiratory system and increase the ability to work harder for longer. However, a long or hard run one day should be followed by a shorter or easier 'recovery' run the next day.

The American College of Sports Medicine's position on the quantity and quality of exercise for developing cardio-respiratory fitness (2011) recommends that most adults engage in moderate-intensity cardio-respiratory exercise training for up to thirty minutes a day on five days per week for a total of 150 minutes per week, vigorous-intensity cardio-respiratory exercise training for up to twenty minutes a day on three days per week (up to seventy-five minutes per week), or a combination of moderate- and vigorous-intensity exercise (light- to moderate-intensity for unconditioned persons initially). The type of exercise should be that which involves major muscle groups and is continuous and rhythmical (Garber et al., 2011).

If we want to measure a person's fitness we usually measure their aerobic capacity. This is known as Maximum Oxygen Uptake (VO_2 Max). It is a measure of the maximum (Max) volume (V) of oxygen (O_2) which can be extracted from the atmosphere, supplied to, and taken up by the tissue cells per minute. The result may be expressed in litres per minute (L/min) or in millilitres of oxygen per kilogram of body weight per minute (ml/kg/min).

VO_2 Max can be measured directly or indirectly. Direct measurement usually involves working a person on a treadmill, collecting and analyzing the expired (breathed out) gasses to calculate exactly how much oxygen is being consumed at various progressions of intensity and when the person reaches his or her maximum intensity. Obviously this requires working the person to maximum and is usually carried out on very fit athletes.

For less fit individuals we can perform a sub-maximal exercise test and estimate their VO_2 Max. Again, we work the person on a treadmill or cycle ergometer and monitor his or her heart rate against a known and progressively increasing intensity (scientists have previously established a very strong correlation between heart rate and oxygen uptake). The heart rate can be plotted on a graph against heart rate on the vertical axis and both workload and oxygen uptake on the horizontal axis. The performer only works to about 75 per cent or 85 per cent of his or her age-related maximum heart rate (220 minus age). We can then join up the points on the graph (linear regression) and extrapolate (continue the straight line) to a horizontal representing their age-related Max HR (heart rate), drop a vertical to the bottom horizontal axis to indicate how much oxygen would be consumed *if* they had worked to maximum. The result in millilitres can then be divided by the person's body weight to give a resulting VO_2 Max in ml/kg/min.

Many modern health clubs provide a computer-assisted fitness testing service where tests include blood pressure, lung function (of which peak expiratory flow is one element), body fat measurement, aerobic fitness and flexibility. For measuring the aerobic fitness a sub-maximal exercise test is carried out and the computer uses the linear regression/extrapolation method described above and illustrated in Fig. 5.1.

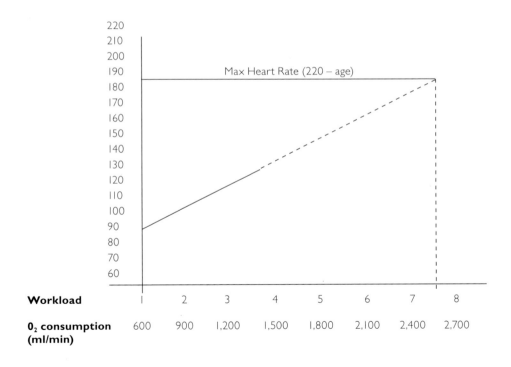

Fig. 5.1 Example: graph showing heart rate monitored against workload, extrapolation, and calculated VO_2 Max. Forty-year-old, weight 70kg: oxygen consumption if worked to max HR (level 7.5) = 2550 ml/min (36.4 ml/kg/min).

Determining Intensity

We have spoken about training intensity, but what exactly do we mean, and how do we measure and determine intensity? Intensity refers to how hard we are working. For aerobic conditioning we need to work hard enough to be above an aerobic threshold, yet not so hard that we go above an anaerobic threshold.

Aerobic threshold is the minimum level of exercise intensity below which there is no beneficial physical conditioning effect derived from the activity. It is generally considered that a minimum of 55 per cent or 65 per cent of maximum heart rate corresponds to aerobic threshold.

Anaerobic threshold is the level of intensity whereby we can no longer supply enough oxygen to the working muscles and energy production depends predominantly on metabolism of fuels without oxygen, resulting in the accumulation of lactic acid in the muscles and the blood. Anaerobic threshold usually occurs somewhere between 80 and 90 per cent of maximum heart rate.

To benefit from aerobic conditioning exercise we have to be working hard enough to raise a sweat and increase heart rate and respiration considerably, yet not so hard as to become exhausted too soon.

One of the easiest guides to exercise intensity is **Rating of Perceived Exertion (RPE)**. Quite simply, this suggests we should be able to judge how hard is the exercise at any one time by the way it actually feels. An experienced athlete can often be very precise using RPE and can perceive when he/she is at anaerobic threshold. Experienced runners can usually judge at what pace they are running in minutes per mile, or can judge a comfortable aerobic recovery pace the day after a hard race. With experience, any runner should be able to perceive (feel and judge) how hard they are working.

RPE scales have been devised for use in physiotherapy centres and sports science laboratories. The original and accepted RPE scale is also known as the 'Borg' Scale.

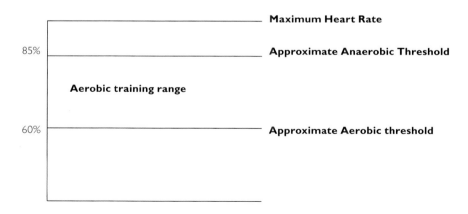

Fig. 5.2   Aerobic and anaerobic thresholds illustrated as a percentage of maximum heart rate.

It uses a scale from 6 to 20 with certain numbers representing different exercise intensities depending on how the performer feels. If asked how hard the exercise feels, the performer can simply give a number.

A variation on the Borg Scale was introduced for clinical conditions and uses a numerical range from 0 to 10 (see Fig. 5.3). It could be employed by runners who should aim for a level of 3 or 4 to achieve a conditioning effect.

0	Nothing at all
1	Very light
2	Fairly light
3	Moderate
4	Somewhat hard
5	Hard
6	
7	Very hard
8	
9	
10	Very, very hard

Fig. 5.3   The 11-point (0–10) Borg Scale of Rating of Perceived Exertion.

Determining Target Heart Rates

Another accurate and useful guide to exercise intensity, especially with aerobic conditioning, is heart rate. We can calculate and work to a **percentage of Maximum Heart Rate (Max HR, or MHR)**. To determine MHR we either have to exercise to maximum or use a simple calculation to provide a general indication.

Exercising to maximum to determine achievable MHR may be acceptable, and indeed necessary, for a well-trained athlete, but is not advisable for beginners running for health-related fitness. They would be advised to use the simple calculation whereby we subtract our age from 220.

220 beats per minute is considered to be the highest that any human heart can beat and may be possible in a very young baby. It is then considered that this reduces by approximately one beat per minute (bpm) for every year of age, hence the calculation **220 – age = MHR**. Once we have calculated our age-related MHR we can then find a percentage of that maximum at which to train and this is then referred to as **Training or Target Heart Rate (THR)**.

Example: A 30-year-old individual to work at 70 per cent age-related MHR:

220 – 30 = 190 bpm (MHR)
190 x 70 per cent = 133 bpm (THR)

The following chart is very often displayed in the gymnasium as a quick guide to exercise intensity and is based on the formula, 220 – age = Max HR × per cent.

Exercise intensities (and therefore the chart below) can be divided into a number of training zones according to the purpose of the training session and the ability of the performer:

60–70 per cent = fat burning zone
70–80 per cent = aerobic training zone
80–90 per cent = competitive training zone

The competitive training zone may also be referred to as the anaerobic threshold zone, because at some stage within this zone the

Heart Rate

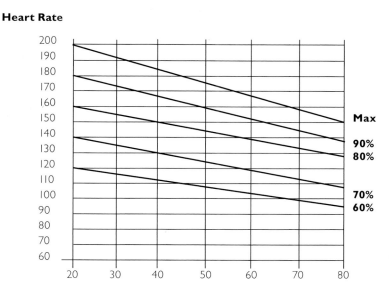

Fig. 5.4   Training/target heart rate chart.

majority of people will cross their anaerobic threshold. This is the exercise intensity whereby energy production moves from being predominantly aerobic to anaerobic. At this intensity, because of insufficient oxygen, lactic acid starts to accumulate in the muscle and the blood and the intensity cannot continue for very long.

Anaerobic threshold is generally considered to correspond with the exercise intensity whereby lactic acid levels reach 4 m.mol/litre in blood (Maughan, 1990; Williams, 1990).

As a general guide an aerobic training range would be between about 65 per cent and 85 per cent of maximum. Beginners would be advised to work closer to the lower end of that range (65–75 per cent) and may actually become anaerobic well before 80 per cent. Fitter individuals may be capable of training at higher intensities (75–85 per cent) and

remain basically aerobic. Trained athletes can exceed 85 per cent and still rely mainly on aerobic energy pathways. Also genetics can influence a person's ability to run aerobically at higher intensities.

Readers may have realized that at a given intensity the performer is working at a percentage of his/her VO_2 Max. Aerobic training will be between approximately 55 per cent or 60 per cent to 80 per cent or 85 per cent VO_2 Max, which very roughly correlates with the above-mentioned range for THR.

For trained athletes and older fitter individuals the 220 minus age calculation may not be accurate as they are often capable of achieving a higher MHR than this calculation dictates. Such subjects would have to actually exercise to maximum and determine an achievable MHR. From this they could then calculate a percentage at which to train (THR).

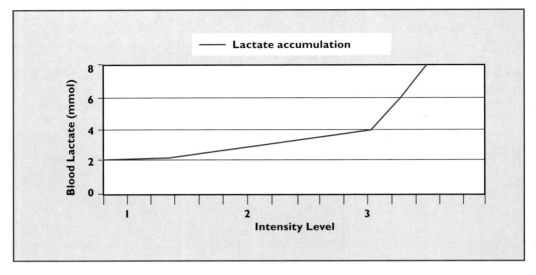

Fig. 5.5   *Lactate accumulation with increase in intensity.*

Example: 30-year-old trained athlete to work at 70 per cent *achievable* MHR:

Achievable MHR = <u>194</u> bpm (NB: 220 – 30
= only 190 × 70 per cent = 133 bpm)
194 × 70 per cent = 136 bpm (THR)

For the fitter person it may be more accurate to use the Karvonen method, which considers heart rate range, and resting heart rate (RHR) enters the equation. We subtract RHR from MHR, calculate the desired percentage of that result and add back to that result the RHR, which then gives us the THR.

Example: A very fit 30-year-old athlete to work at 70 per cent MHR:

RHR = 45 bpm
220 – age = 190 bpm (MHR)
190 (MHR) – 45 (RHR) = 145
145 × 70 per cent = 102
102 + 45 = 147 bpm (THR)

It can be seen that the result, 147 bpm (THR), is considerably higher than the previous 133 or 136 bpm (THR). However, we could be even more accurate. The above example employed the 220-minus-age method of determining MHR. If we use the Karvonen method but use *achievable MHR*, the result is as follows:

Achievable MHR = 194 bpm
194 (MHR) – 45 (RHR) = 149
149 × 70 per cent = 104
104 + 45 = 149 bpm (THR)

How do we measure resting heart rate (RHR)? First of all we must understand that RHR refers to a true resting heart rate, which means we are at rest and not moving about. It is often suggested that the best time to measure a RHR by counting a pulse is as soon as we wake up in the morning. If we were to do that over four or five days and average it out we should get an indication of our RHR. I have also found a good time to measure RHR

A simple guide to exercise intensity whereby the performer should be working aerobically (and the beginner safely) is to run at a pace at which you could hold a conversation. If you can speak you will be in an aerobic state. If you become so breathless that you cannot speak you will be working anaerobically, which will be too high an intensity, may not be safe, and the activity will not continue for much longer.

Obviously the 220-minus-age method, where we calculate a percentage of the resulting maximum (referred to as *age-related MHR*) is much safer for beginners. It provides a safe guide to intensities that should be effective.

General Guidelines for Running Intensity

For running, as an aerobic conditioning activity, to be both safe and effective we must consider the **FIT factors: Frequency, Intensity** and **Time** (duration). Any one, or all three, can vary and change as the body progressively adapts and fitness improves.

is mid-afternoon, if the opportunity arises – a few hours after the previous meal, lying down for about half an hour, in comfortably cool conditions. If a heart rate monitor is worn it will give a very accurate read-out.

Regarding frequency, intensity and time, the following is generally recommended:

For the control of body weight, and for the development and maintenance of a higher aerobic capacity, aerobic conditioning activities should be carried out at least *three times per week*, at a *moderate intensity*, yet high enough to increase heart rate above 65 per cent of maximum and to increase breathing and respiration. Each session should be continuous for a minimum of about *twenty minutes*.

Two walk/jog sessions per week, at a comfortable intensity for twenty minutes per session, might be suitable for a beginner embarking on a training programme after a period of inactivity. As fitness increases in achievable stages, the frequency may increase to three times per week.

Intensity need not increase, except that the walking sections may decrease in length and number and the jogging sections increase in length and number.

Depending on the runner's objectives (general fitness, weight loss/control, racing), intensity may eventually increase, yet still be within the performer's aerobic limitations, and duration may progressively increase up to sixty minutes per session.

CHAPTER 6

PHYSIOLOGICAL ADAPTATIONS TO TRAINING

Running produces an aerobic conditioning effect. As an aerobic activity it brings about many beneficial adaptations in the systems of the body. Adaptations are long-term changes that usually result in an improvement in the function of the tissues.

These adaptations occur mainly in the tissues of the muscular system, the cardiovascular system and the respiratory system. Their combined effect results in an increased aerobic capacity, a general reduction in blood pressure, and affords some protection against the development of coronary heart disease and heart attack, as will be discussed in more detail later in this chapter.

Muscular Adaptations

The influence of aerobic conditioning exercise is mainly on the Type I (red/slow twitch/ aerobic) fibres, but it can also impact on the Type IIa (white/fast twitch/intermediate) fibres.

There is an increase in the number and size of mitochondria and an increase in myoglobin, which improve the muscles' ability to take up and process oxygen. There is an increase in the number of capillaries (small blood vessels) allowing an increased blood supply to the muscles and a greater capacity for cellular oxygen uptake. Also within the muscle there is an increase in aerobic enzymes (substances

which cause metabolism [use] of fuels with oxygen) and a resulting increase in the ability to mobilize fat and use it as fuel. Equally important is the improvement in the ability to process waste products.

Training at higher intensities yet within the aerobic threshold can influence the Type IIa (intermediate) fibres. Adaptations in these fibres increase their ability to take up and process oxygen, thus increasing muscular endurance at higher intensities.

Cardiovascular Adaptations

Heart

Chronic adaptations as a result of regular aerobic exercise include left ventricular hypertrophy, and an increase in left ventricular volume. This will result in a stronger, more efficient and more effective heart muscle (myocardial hypertrophy), an increase in stroke volume (the amount of blood per heart beat), a decrease in resting heart rate, and a decrease in working heart rate for a given workload.

Also contributing to an increase in stroke volume is the increase in contractility of the heart muscle. The heart has the ability to contract with greater force and becomes a more effective pump.

One particularly important training effect on the heart is the increase in myocardial capillaries. This will result in an increased capacity for myocardial oxygen uptake (Scheuer and Tipton, 1977). In addition to this increase in the number of capillaries, the coronary arteries that supply nourishment and oxygen to the heart muscle can become larger and comparatively free from atheroma (fatty deposits).

Blood vessels

There is an improvement in arterial elasticity and therefore less resistance to blood flow with a reduction in blood pressure. Also contributing to the reduction in blood pressure is the increase in capillaries which occurs in the skeletal muscles and heart muscle (myocardium).

Blood

Circulatory adaptations include an increase in blood volume, an increase in red blood cells and haemoglobin, and therefore an increased capacity for oxygen transportation. Within the blood there is a change in the ratio of low density lipoprotein (LDL) to high density lipoprotein (HDL). This is facilitated by an increase in HDL, resulting in a more effective transportation and suspension of cholesterol, less adherence to the artery wall, and therefore protection against coronary and systemic atherosclerosis (hardening of the arteries) (Ashton and Davies, 1986).

Increased fibrinolysis reduces the tendency for the blood to clot, while increased levels of prostaglandins reduce platelet aggregation, and the overall effect reduces blood coagulation (Ashton and Davies, 1986).

Respiratory Adaptations

Respiratory adaptations include an increase in the number and size of lung alveoli (the smallest parts of the lung where oxygen is absorbed). This will result in an increased capacity for oxygen uptake. There is also an increase in pulmonary capillaries, which again will improve gaseous exchange and oxygen diffusion.

The diaphragm, intercostal muscles and other respiratory muscles increase in strength and therefore both relaxed and forced breathing becomes easier.

The Combined Effects of Aerobic Conditioning

As aerobic exercise produces long-term and beneficial adaptations in the muscular, cardiovascular and respiratory systems, the combined effect is an increase in the body's ability to take in, deliver and take up oxygen.

The whole cardio-respiratory system (heart, lungs, blood vessels and blood), together with the muscles' ability to take up oxygen, can be compared to a railway system transporting passengers between two stations.

The passengers to be transported are the oxygen molecules which enter the lungs station. They stand on the *alveoli* platform awaiting the train. The engine is the *heart*, the carriages are the *red blood cells*, and the carriage seats are the *haemoglobin* molecules.

At the *lungs station*, as the *oxygen passengers get on* to the train, the *carbon dioxide passengers (having travelled from the muscle station), get off* the train and on to the alveoli platform before exiting the station.

The train then transports the oxygen passengers to the muscle station, where they disembark onto the *mitochondria* platform. At the same time, carbon dioxide passengers from the mitochondria platform get on to the train to be transported back to the lungs (see Fig. 6.1).

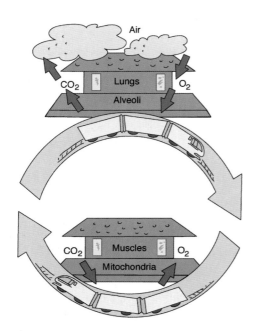

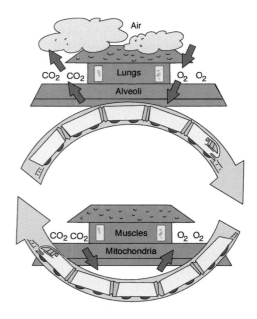

Fig. 6.1   The cardio-respiratory system compared to a railway system. (Original concept: Bob Smith, M.Ed., Department of Physical Education and Sport Science, Loughborough University)

Fig. 6.2   The cardio-respiratory system improved by aerobic conditioning. (Original concept: Bob Smith, M.Ed., Department of Physical Education and Sport Science, Loughborough University)

Aerobic exercise improves the whole system: At the lungs station the *alveoli platform increases in size, accommodating more oxygen passengers*. For the train the heart engine increases in size and strength, and pulls *more red blood cell carriages with more haemoglobin*. Therefore it can carry *more oxygen and carbon dioxide* passengers. At the muscle station there is a *bigger mitochondria platform*, again able to accommodate *more oxygen and carbon dioxide passengers* (see Fig. 6.2).

The result, if we recall Dr Cooper's definition of fitness discussed in the Introduction, is a much fitter body with an increased ability to transport, take up and utilize oxygen. This is one of the major health-related benefits of aerobic exercise, not only making the body

more efficient and effective at performing physical tasks, but also contributing towards the prevention of many undesirable chronic conditions, illnesses and diseases.

Adaptations in the muscular system that increase the muscles' ability to utilize oxygen and metabolize fat occur as a result of long-term aerobic training. The result is an increase, not only in VO_2 Max, but also in anaerobic threshold. Anaerobic threshold is regarded as that point during physical exertion whereby oxygen supply cannot completely fulfil the demand for energy production. Glycogen becomes the main fuel, and lactate starts to accumulate in the blood.

Another term for anaerobic threshold is Onset of Blood Lactate Accumulation (OBLA). It is generally considered that OBLA occurs when lactate concentrations in the blood reach 4 m.mol/l (Maughan, 1990; Williams, 1990).

As aerobic training has the effect of improving the muscles' ability to produce energy with oxygen, the intensity required for lactate concentrations to reach 4 m.mol/l increases.

Aerobic Exercise and Cardio-protection

It is generally agreed by most physical educationalists, sports therapists and medical practitioners that regular physical exercise, particularly of aerobic conditioning exercise, provides a degree of protection for the cardiovascular system against the development of coronary heart disease and heart attack.

Epidemiological evidence has accumulated over four to five decades, along with the evidence concerning the anatomical, biochemical and physiological changes which take place as a result of regular exercise, and how these changes may influence other risk factors. Some of the most important studies took place during the 1950s, '60s, '70s and '80s.

Davis et al. (1988) listed physical inactivity as one of the coronary heart disease risk factors that can be altered by lifestyle changes, and as evidence in favour of the cardio-protective nature of exercise discussed population studies including Morris's (1953, 1973) studies, and Brunner's (1960) study of kibbutz workers. They also discussed the chronic physiological changes that take place to improve the cardiovascular system.

A large number of reports have indicated that populations or individuals with high levels of physical activity tend to have a lower prevalence of symptomatic coronary artery disease and lower death rate from cardiovascular disease.

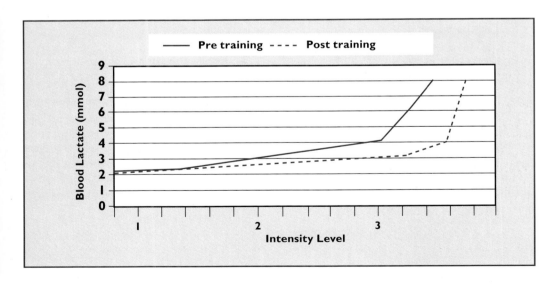

Fig. 6.3   The increase in anaerobic threshold, or OBLA, as a result of long-term aerobic training (lactate/workload curve shifts to the right).

Morris et al. (1953) carried out the London Transport Study. This was one of the first large-scale studies of activity and heart disease. Over a period of two years a study took place of the drivers and conductors of the Central red buses, trams and trolley buses, and a one-year study of guards and motormen of the underground railways.

In each category of transportation there was a considerable difference in work-related activity levels between drivers and conductors, guards and motormen. It was found that the more active conductors had 50 per cent fewer heart attacks than the more sedentary drivers, and also that any heart conditions suffered by the conductors tended to be less serious and later in life. The railway workers' activity levels were similar to the bus and tram workers, and heart disease patterns were also similar.

At the same time, Morris et al. (1953) carried out a parallel study of postal workers and civil servants. The postal workers, being more active than the clerical and executive civil servants, showed a lower incidence of heart disease, and any heart disease in the postal workers was less severe than in the sedentary group.

Morris (1973) carried out the British Civil Servants Study. Two decades after the original Transport Workers Study, a study was carried out of the leisure-time activity levels of executive civil servants across Britain. The incidence of heart attack was considerably less in those engaging in vigorous leisure-time activity than in those reporting no vigorous activity.

The emphasis on leisure-time activity was because of the changing occupational activity levels as a result of labour-saving technology. Also Morris (1973) emphasized vigorous activity in order to determine a threshold level at which the exercise had a beneficial effect. Those workers who partook in light activity showed little cardio-protective benefit from the exercise. Morris (1973) determined not simply that exercise had a beneficial effect, but that the intensity and duration had an important influence. He concluded that exercise did have a beneficial cardiovascular effect and a cardio-protective effect, and stated that 'the generality of the advantage suggests that vigorous exercise is a natural defence of the body, with a protective effect on the ageing heart against ischaemia and its consequences'.

In the USA, Paffenbarger and Hale (1975) carried out the San Francisco Dock Workers Study. Some 6,351 subjects were studied for a period of twenty-two years (1951–72). The categories of work involved some in heavy work, some in moderate work, and some in light work. The majority of deaths from heart disease were in the light work category, with moderate work next, and the least number of deaths in the heavy work category.

Paffenbarger and Hale (1975) also took into account other risk factors that showed exercise as an independent risk factor. This study also showed the importance of threshold levels of exercise intensity. Below a certain level, exercise had little effect.

Paffenbarger, Wing and Hyde (1978) carried out the Harvard University Alumni Study. The sporting activity levels of 16,936 former male students, aged thirty-five to seventy-four years, were studied and categorized into light or strenuous sport. The results indicated that a cardio-protective effect was gained by those involved in the high level of energy expenditure across the entire age range studied.

Once again, a threshold level was shown to exist, and that subjects who were active as students yet sedentary in later life achieved little cardio-protection. Benefit was only achieved by those who remained active.

Sharkey (1975) referred briefly to a number of population studies that suggested a cardio-protective effect from exercise. He quoted

Zukel, Lewis and Enterline (1959), and Fox and Haskell (1968). Sharkey stated that one hour of heavy physical activity daily lowered the incidence of coronary heart disease to less than 20 per cent of the sedentary rate, the incidence of heart attack to 50 per cent, and the deaths from heart disease were reduced to less than half of the sedentary rate, depending on the study chosen, the population investigated, and the level of physical activity involved.

More recent studies and reviews support the contribution of regular physical activity to cardio-protection with recommendations concerning amounts and intensities (Nelson et al., 2007; Gielen, 2010; Hamer et al., 2012).

Aerobic Adaptations and Cardio-protection

Most of the adaptations discussed previously in this chapter have a direct and indirect beneficial effect on the heart. The increased stroke volume causes a reduced resting heart rate and a reduced working heart rate, which reduces the amount of work required by the heart muscle for a given work load. Increased cardiac and muscle, capillaries with increased arterial elasticity should reduce arterial blood pressure. A reduction in blood pressure reduces the amount of strain on the heart muscle.

Consistently high levels of blood pressure (hypertension) are recognized as a major risk factor for heart disease and heart attack. Regular aerobic exercise, due to the adaptations it affords, is one factor that can help reduce elevated blood pressure (Bonanno and Lies, 1974; McArdle et al., 1991).

Bonanno and Lies (1974) studied the effects of physical training on coronary risk factors in thirty-nine middle-aged men who were at high risk of coronary artery disease. They found that exercise training led to a substantial improvement in physical fitness as determined by increased maximal oxygen uptake, ventilation and physical work capacity. There was a significant reduction of systolic blood pressure in the hypertensive subjects who exercised, but not in the hypertensive control subjects. Diastolic pressure decreased in both groups.

Ashton and Davies (1986) also reported that aerobic exercise increases fibrinolysis, which reduces the tendency of the blood to clot, and this may be one important mechanism of prevention and protection against heart attack. They also reported evidence that exercise may increase levels of prostaglandin, which has been shown to inhibit the aggregation of platelets.

Evidence is available that physical inactivity has a greater impact on the development of heart disease than the combined effect of smoking, high blood pressure and diabetes (Haskel et al., 2007; Warren et al., 2010; Chomistek et al., 2012).

> The mass of evidence from both epidemiological and physiological studies appears overwhelming in support of the argument that regular vigorous aerobic exercise produces many beneficial changes in the body, which in turn afford a degree of cardio-protection.

Aerobic Exercise, Weight Control and Weight Reduction

Aerobic exercise/training is weight-controlling simply because we can work for longer periods of time, more frequently and in the long-term burn more calories. It is true that during exercise at lower intensities we are burning a higher proportion of fat as fuel. Fat is stored in adipose tissue at various sites on the body and is converted to free fatty acids which can then be transported in the blood stream to the working muscles and used as fuel to be metabolized with a plentiful supply of oxygen to produce energy. Many runners have believed that running at a lower intensity is better for weight reduction because it burns the fat which we are trying to reduce. This is not actually the case. What really matters is that we burn enough calories over a period of time, and whether they are burned as fat or carbohydrate does not matter. It is the total amount of long-term calorie expenditure that matters, not the type of fuel metabolized (Westaway, 1991).

Running at lower intensities *will* be effective in weight reduction because the performer can run for long enough and frequently enough to burn enough calories per day, per week, per month, etc. Working at higher intensities can also burn the same number of calories depending on the duration and frequency. However, this is not recommended for the less fit individual or beginner.

What is important is safety, effectiveness and the performer's fitness level, along with adherence to a running regime. For the beginner who may be trying to lose body weight, lower intensities are much safer.

In addition, the lower intensity makes the running more tolerable and less painful, which should contribute towards the pleasure and therefore adherence. Very often on THR charts the lower intensities (65 per cent to 75 per cent of MHR) are marked as the *fat-burning zone*. This is correct, but sometimes it

is marked as *weight management zone*, which is not necessarily correct. The performer should keep in mind that by working at the lower intensities he/she has to work longer to burn enough calories. In defence of the term weight management zone, it is true, however, that when working at a low intensity the performer can work for longer periods of time and therefore ultimately burn more calories.

Running at a lower intensity helps to control/reduce body weight because, by metabolizing mainly fat with oxygen, toxic waste products do not accumulate in the blood stream and the working muscles. This allows the performer to continue the activity for longer periods of time and consequently burn more calories.

For less-fit beginners, very low intensities allow a longer duration of exercise, as their bodies are not yet effective or efficient at removing waste products of metabolism. Even at moderate intensities the accumulation of lactic acid may build up in the tissues and elicit premature cessation of the activity.

The bottom line is that to lose weight, more calories must be expended than are taken in, so beware appetite increase with exercise if weight loss is the aim.

CHAPTER 7

RUNNING TECHNIQUE

Everybody has a unique, individual style of walking or running. People can often be recognized from a distance or from behind by their particular style of movement. Running style is natural to the individual, but there may be modifications which can be made to improve running posture, increase energy efficiency and reduce the potential risk of injury.

Correct, or recommended, technique comes naturally to some individuals, but may have to be developed by others. Actually, there is no absolutely correct technique, but there may be certain aspects of running technique which can be considered and put into practice that improve efficiency and reduce the risk of injury.

Posture and Technique

- Run with an upright posture. This should align the body, assist relaxation and improve balance. It will also assist effective breathing and will reduce fatigue in certain postural muscles.
- Be relaxed, especially around the shoulders and arms (do not clench the fists or hunch the shoulders). Negative tension wastes valuable energy and can result in aching muscles and discomfort.
- Keep your head up and in line with your spine. This helps to maintain an upright posture and also allows good observation.

Be observant at all times – many hazards exist, such as lamp posts, kerbstones, tree roots, dogs, wheelie bins, vehicles, etc.

- Your hips should be over your feet; do not allow the pelvis to tilt which can result in stiffness in the lower back.
- Do not lift your knees too high (despite onlookers shouting 'knees up'!)
- Keep the knees 'soft' (slightly bent) as your feet make contact with the ground. 'Soft' knees provide natural 'cushioning' to reduce impact on landing.
- Elbows should be bent at right angles and the arms relaxed. The arms move to and fro, opposite to the legs, to counter rotation.
- Use your abdominal muscles to hold in the tummy, helping to maintain a good, upright posture. Do not tense and strain. It needs to be instinctive and relaxed and may be achieved progressively through regularly performing core stability exercises (see Chapter 8).
- Breathing should be instinctively relaxed, rhythmical and in time with your running tempo. Without being overly conscious of it, try to develop a breathing rate which complements your running pace. For someone new to running, it might take a while for this to develop as muscles adapt and improve their ability to take up oxygen from the blood. I tend to breathe in for two steps and out for two steps.

Foot Strike

It used to be believed that when running we landed heel first (heel strike). A 'heel-toe' technique was even taught and recommended. However, many runners do not actually heel strike, but land more on the mid- to fore-foot.

If we heel strike with a fairly straight leg, an equivalent force of up to twelve times our body weight can be transmitted up through the body, which can affect ankles, knees, hips and spine (McDougal, 2009). It also creates a braking action.

Prior to the first specific running shoe appearing in the 1970s, runners wore thin-soled canvas shoes with little, or no, cushioning. Motion control had not even been thought of. Runners landed on their fore-foot with slightly bent knees. Foot strike was on the outer side of the fore-foot and then the foot rolled and the weight was transferred to the inner side of the foot to push off the big toe region. This is pronation – a natural action of a healthy, strong foot (more about the so-called 'evils' of over-pronation later).

The top runners in history were fore-foot strikers. They had to be, and this was/is natural. The structures of a strong foot are designed to absorb shock, cushion and control motion. Heel striking has a braking action, whereas fore-foot running allows a flowing movement.

The forward foot moves towards the ground in a downward, backward, 'stroking' motion (not punching or pounding) and the outer edge of the ball of the foot makes first contact with the ground. Running progression results from these forces pushing behind the centre of gravity of the body (McDougal, 2009, citing Fred Wilt, 1959, in *How They Train*).

Most runners never think about their running style or technique. I would advise all runners, whatever their level or experience, to think about their running style. They may be surprised to find they are naturally fore-foot-striking. Observe other runners and you will probably notice the same. Now, possibly for the first time, be aware of your style. Be prepared to make very slight modifications (yes, you can teach an old dog new tricks!); think about the fore-foot contacting (not slapping) the ground and pushing backwards; be conscious of a slight bend at the knees; feel the natural springy cushioning.

Try this – shorten your stride slightly. Concentrate on landing on the outer side of the mid- to fore-foot. Keep your knees soft. Foot strike should be directly underneath and in line with the hips. Keep your body upright and look ahead. Elbows should be at right-angles with a gentle swing and shoulders relaxed.

Do not over-stride – if you do, foot-strike will be too far in front of the hips. Be aware of a backward push as you propel yourself forward (think of a fighting bull scraping the ground with its hoof before it charges, or have in mind a 'circular' leg action similar to cycling). You should feel light and comfortable. An increase in pace is achieved by a faster leg turnover, not by lengthening your stride.

The idea behind the modern running shoe, with gel, air, rubber, or other scientifically devised material under the heel, was to allow runners to heel strike and achieve a longer stride in the belief that it could make them faster. However, it did not, and possibly resulted in more injuries than it 'prevented'.

I watched Alistair Brownlee winning gold

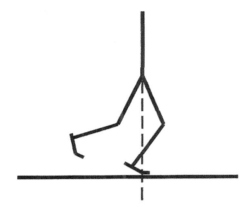

Fig. 7.1   Mid- or fore-foot strike: comparatively short stride; foot strike under the hips; knees 'soft'.

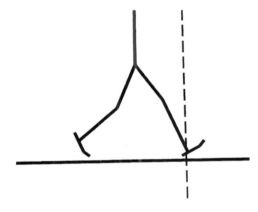

Fig. 7.2   Heel strike: foot strike well in front of the hips; straighter front leg; creates a braking effect.

for Great Britain in the 2012 Olympic Games Men's Triathlon. As he completed the run towards the finish line his fore-foot, soft-knee running style was a delight to watch. He was 'floating' – so light, poetry in motion.

In his book, *Born To Run* (2009), McDougal also considers the blade, devised to enable lower leg amputees to run. There is no heel. The 'C'-shape mimics the same action as a fore-foot strike. (Having used the term 'fore-foot', more appropriate might be 'mid-foot'. Douglas [2013] suggested that a true fore-foot landing is rare and can be as inefficient as heavy heel landing. Somewhere between a slight heel landing and mid-foot is best for most people.)

Why is it that the outer edge of the heel of the modern running shoe wears down if we fore-foot strike? Probably because the depth of the heel causes it to contact the floor as we land on the outer side of the fore-foot. As we fore-foot-strike, the shoe's heel will contact the ground almost simultaneously, or fractionally afterwards (much of the literature about fore-foot striking suggests allowing the heel to come down gently a fraction after foot-strike and before the foot rolls). It becomes almost a 'flat-foot' landing on the outer side and so there will be some heel contact with the ground on the outer edge.

Shod or au Naturel?

The barefoot running movement is making considerable strides (pardon the pun!) across the world, with runners realizing that the best running 'shoe' is the human foot. A vast network of nerves allow us to 'feel' the ground, and the many bones, joints, tendons and ligaments absorb impact, roll the foot and, combined with 'soft' knees, provide spring.

Unfortunately, no sooner do we take our first precarious and wobbly steps as a baby, we are put in shoes. Shoes carry out most of the work that the tissues and structures of the foot are supposed to perform. Consequently, our feet become weaker. The foot's arch is the strongest and most effective load-bearing structure ever devised. Any builder or engineer knows how very strong an arch is, especially if load is applied from above. However, shoes exert an upward force on the foot's arch and it weakens.

In hotter climates people spend a lot of time in bare feet. Their feet develop strength as nature intended, able to do the job for which they were designed. I had a university house-mate who was born and raised in South Africa and hardly wore shoes until he came to England as a teenager. Also, the South African runner, Zola Budd, had never run in shoes until she was brought to England in the 1980s and hurriedly made a UK citizen in order to represent Great Britain at athletics.

In colder climates we entomb our feet in leather, with raised heels, arch supports and cushioning. Our feet become lazy and weak. The more cushioning, the less the feet have to do and the weaker they become. As runners, we have become dependent on heel cushioning, torsion devices, motion control, mid-sole densities, anti-pronation material and orthotics. The technology in the modern running shoe has taken over the role for which the foot was designed but has lost the ability to fulfil.

I am not singing the praises of barefoot running, nor necessarily advising it. It may be fine for those in warmer climates and those with naturally strong feet. Like anything new, a person who has always walked and run in shoes cannot suddenly change. A lot of strengthening, toning and flexibility training would be required.

It is developing a considerable following in Australia and parts of the USA, with many distance runners either completely unshod or wearing specifically designed 'minimalist' running shoes, which consist merely of a strip of thin protective rubber under the sole and a material top – and cost a fortune! Even some top American track stars incorporate a barefoot session into their training.

I would advise any running beginner to consider purchasing 'proper' running shoes. If possible, go to a specialist running shop and seek advice. Some may have a treadmill on which you can run while being filmed from behind and your gait is then 'assessed' (I use the word 'assessed' with caution as I question the qualification of some shop assistants to accurately interpret the result, diagnose foot problems and analyze foot motion). Remember they are in business to sell shoes. You might be advised that you need a good motion control /anti-pronation shoe, but the most expensive is not necessarily the best.

Motion control – usually anti-pronation – consists of different densities of material in the medial (inner) aspect of the shoe's mid-sole, intended to reduce the amount of inward roll of the foot. The word 'pronation' has developed a bad name with runners. However, pronation is a natural and necessary movement of the foot where weight is transferred from the outer edge of the foot to the inner aspect of the fore-foot for push-off. Weakness in the foot, with dropped arches, known as a flat foot (pes planus), can cause the foot to over-pronate. Over-pronation can cause abnormal stress to ankles, knees, hips and/or the spine.

Regular, long-time runners have usually found the shoe that suits them and with which they are happy. Stick with it if it feels right and gives you confidence, but, once again, the most expensive is not necessarily the best. Sometimes, with more technology, the running shoe can over-compensate for a foot weakness and cause stress to be applied elsewhere. Orthotics compensate for a weakness but do not cure the cause.

I would strongly recommend trying to strengthen the feet (Douglas [2013] also recommends foot strengthening and core stability strengthening). This is something most people will never have considered and it requires a concerted and dedicated effort. It may be that eventually you will have no need for expensive motion control.

There are many exercises which, if performed daily, can help to strengthen and improve all the tissues and structures of the feet. Ligaments and tendons can be strengthened; intrinsic and extrinsic muscles which influence correct foot function can be strengthened; and better flexibility in the joints can be developed.

1. Move the toes/foot and ankle through their normal/intended ranges of movement:

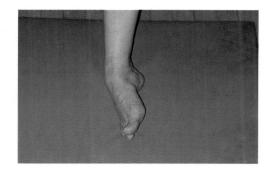

Fig. 7.3c   Inversion.

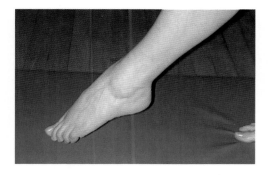

Fig. 7.3a   Plantar-flexion.

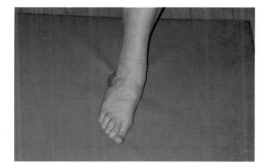

Fig. 7.3d   Eversion.

2. Seated toe clenching (Fig. 7.4): Either simply clench the toes, or place the feet on a towel and try to ruffle up the towel with your toes. Perform ten repetitions.

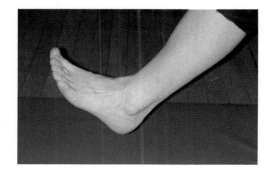

Fig. 7.3b   Dorsi-flexion.

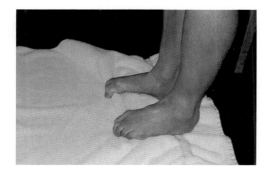

Fig. 7.4   Seated toe clenching.

3. Standing toe clenching (Fig. 7.5): Stand still on two feet and pull the toes backwards along the floor. Perform ten repetitions.

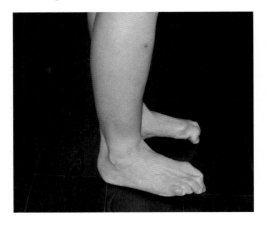

Fig. 7.5   Standing toe clenching.

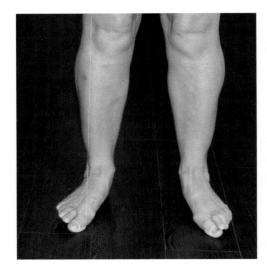

Fig. 7.6 b   Standing rock and roll.

4. Standing rock and roll (Figs 7.6a and b): Stand still on two bare feet; rock onto the outer edge (inversion) and then roll onto the inner edge (eversion). Perform ten repetitions.

5. Rising up onto the toes/lifting the heel (Fig. 7.7): Stand on the floor in bare feet and lift up onto the toes. Perform a number of repetitions (suggest five or ten; do not over-stress the calf muscles).

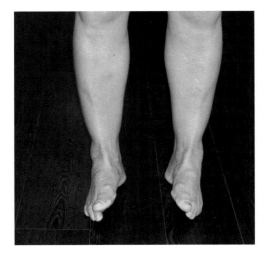

Fig. 7.6a   Standing rock and roll.

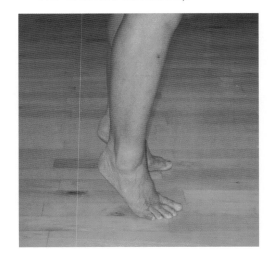

Fig. 7.7   Rising up onto the toes/lifting the heel.

6. Balancing on one leg: Stand on one foot without shoes for as long as possible (aim for twenty to thirty seconds) without having to put down the other foot. Perform on both a hard surface and a soft surface. Use your arms if necessary to help you balance. No need to close your eyes.

   As well as strengthening the intrinsic muscles of the feet, this develops strength and proprioception in the muscles of the lower leg (gastrocnemius and soleus of the calf, posterior tibial muscles immediately behind the shin bone, anterior tibial muscles in front of the shin bone, the peronei on the outer side of the shin), which help to stabilize the ankle.

7. Barefoot walking: Take any opportunity – indoors, or outside in summer – to walk about in bare feet or in very minimalist sandals.

You may experience some aches and pains for a while in the feet, ankles and lower leg. Like any other form of exercise, you are overloading the unaccustomed tissues which then need time to adapt and strengthen. It is worth persevering. Progression must be gradual.

CHAPTER 8

CORE STABILITY AND MAINTENANCE OF POSTURE

Runners should be encouraged to strengthen their core postural muscles, which support the abdomen and spine. Some runners complain of back ache after running, which is possibly caused by a lack of good core stability and poor posture. If the stabilizing muscles of the abdominal region and the spine are weak it can result in an exaggerated lumbar curve, which increases intervertebral disc pressure with resulting muscle spasm and pain.

Maintenance of good running posture can reduce the risk of injury or muscular discomfort. Poor running posture can cause negative tension in muscles around the upper back and shoulders with aching experienced in the neck and shoulder region.

Abdominal Exercise

A vitally important role of the abdominal muscles is core stability. This involves well-toned abdominals employed consciously to stabilize the lumbar spine. Core stability should be achieved in every move we make and in all positions such as standing, sitting, kneeling and when lying both supine and prone. Lumbar stabilization – through awareness of, development of, and employment of, transverse abdominis in particular – forms the basis of all every-day positions and movements including running.

When considering the abdominals, most people merely have in mind the visually obvious rectus abdominis muscle and picture the proverbial 'six pack' stomach as seen in bodybuilders and elite athletes. However, there are many muscles which make up the abdominal group and all play their part in maintaining posture through support and stabilization of the spine.

Rectus abdominis is the more superficial (nearer the surface) muscle with fibres running in a vertical direction. Its origin is on the lower ribs and the insertion is into the pubic bone of the pelvis. Contraction of rectus abdominis flexes the spine.

The internal and external obliques are mainly responsible for rotation of the trunk, with the majority of fibres running diagonally.

Transverse abdominis runs horizontally across the lower abdomen. It does not cross a joint and so does not cause movement. Its role is to stabilize the lumbar spine, and support the abdominal cavity. So awareness of, development of, and control of this muscle is vital. This is the major abdominal muscle involved in core stability or lumbar stabilization and it is essential to develop a knowledge of (a) its existence, and (b) how to and when to achieve transverse abdominal tension.

Fig. 8.1   The abdominal muscles.

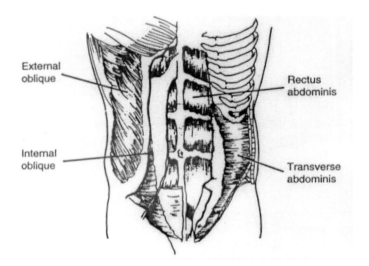

External
oblique

Rectus
abdominis

Internal
oblique

Transverse
abdominis

Exercises should be performed to develop all the abdominal muscles, but it is important that such exercises are safe, achieve exactly what we desire, and do not place excessive stress upon the lumbar spine. They should also be, to some degree, functional. The abdominals should be worked in such a way as to develop effective functioning for everyday activities, support and stabilization.

Unfortunately, with many traditionally practised abdominal exercises the dangers may considerably outweigh the benefits. Full sit-ups, straight leg raises and straight-leg sit-ups, although involving abdominal muscle tension, employ the abdominals in an attempt to stabilize the lumbar spine. With a lot of people, however, the abdominals are not strong enough to carry out that function and the lumbar spine is pulled into hyper-extension by the hip flexor muscles. The spine is therefore subjected to tremendous stress with very high pressure exerted upon the inter-vertebral discs.

If we analyze the movements involved in many traditional abdominal exercises, they involve hip flexion. Such exercises therefore employ the **hip flexor** muscles as prime movers. These muscles have to exert extremely high forces by working against long levers, and therefore work against very heavy resistances. As the **hip flexor** muscles attach to the vertebrae of lumbar spine, the pull on those vertebrae and the force applied to the lumbar spine can be very high.

Suggested Abdominal Exercises

When performing these abdominal exercises, be sure to breathe out on the effort (curl) and breathe in on the return.

Abdominal Curls

Abdominal curls employ the abdominal muscles 100 per cent and impose very little stress upon the lumbar spine.

- *Muscles targeted:* Rectus abdominis, transverse abdominis.
- *Technique:* Lie on your back with the knees bent and feet on the floor. Place the hands either on the thighs (easy), across the chest (harder), or by the side of your head (harder still). Lift the head and shoulders and curl the trunk.

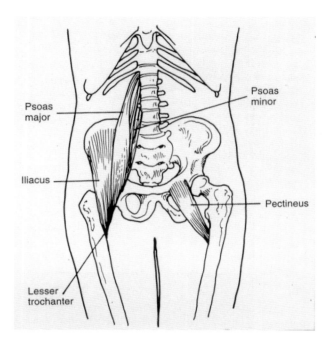

Fig. 8.2   The hip flexor muscles.

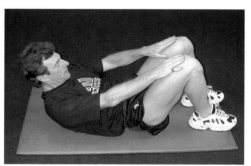

Figs 8.3a, b and c   Abdominal curl progressions:
Increases in resistance intensity can be achieved by
placing the hands on the thighs (a), across the chest
(b), or at the side of the head (c).

- *Safety tip:* Keep the lower back in contact with the floor. Do not place the hands behind the head as there is a tendency to tug and impose stress on the cervical vertebrae of the neck.

Twist Curls

- Muscles targeted: Obliques and rectus abdominis.
- Technique: Knees bent, feet flat on the floor. Place one ankle on the knee of the other leg, hands by the side of the head. Curl up, keeping the lower back in contact with the floor, and twist to bring the left elbow towards the right knee. After a number of repetitions repeat right elbow towards the left knee.
- Safety tip: Keep the lower back on the floor. Keep the elbow/upper arm on the floor to support the spine.

Reverse Curls

Reputedly, reverse curls are performed to work the lower abdominals. In this exercise, it is the pelvis that is lifted and not the legs. NB: A study carried out by Willett et al. (2001) found that reverse curl was the most effective abdominal exercise for working the oblique muscles.

- *Muscles targeted:* Lower abdominals (possibly inferior fibres of rectus abdominis), transverse abdominis, obliques.
- *Technique:* Tuck the knees towards the chest and hold that position. Lift the pelvis so that the hips rise slightly from the floor.
- *Safety tip:* Work comparatively slowly and in control. Do not jerk the movement.

Fig. 8.4 Twist curls (abdominals and obliques).

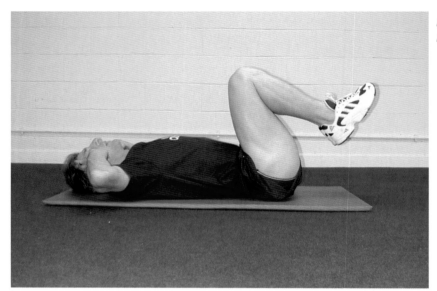

*Figs 8.5a and b
Reverse curls.*

Functional Abdominal Stabilizing Exercises

We also need to perform some functional abdominal stabilizing exercises that work the abdominals by employing contractions of the transverse abdominals as stabilizers.

1. First of all, practise the neutral position. Pull the tummy in to stabilize the spine, which should have just a slight arch in the lumbar region. Practise breathing without allowing the tummy to bulge.

2. Breathe out and at the same time slide one leg out. Return that leg while breathing in. Repeat with the other leg. This causes some contraction of the abdominal muscles in order to stabilize the lumbar spine.

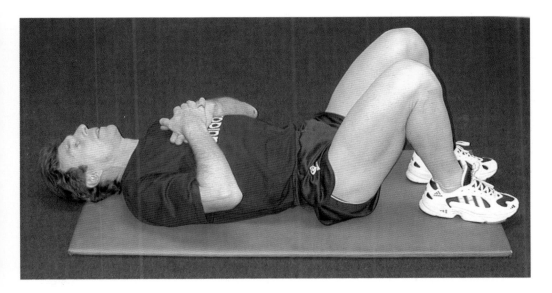

Fig. 8.6   1. Neutral position.

Fig. 8.7   2. Easiest action.

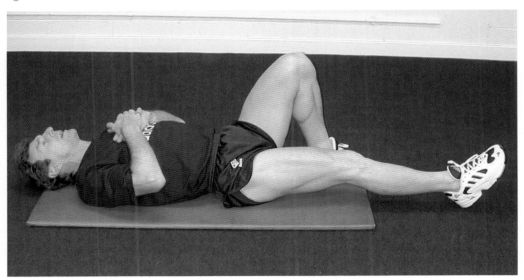

3. Perform an abdominal curl, lifting the head and shoulders, flexing the spine, and breathing out at the same time as the leg slides out. Breathe in as the leg is returned and the head and shoulders are lowered and then repeat with the other leg.

4. Have the hips flexed so that the thighs are vertical and the knees over the hips. Now move out and lower one leg while breathing out. Return that leg while breathing in and then repeat with the other leg.

Fig. 8.8   3. Progression.

Fig. 8.9   4. Further progression.

5. To progress even further, perform an abdominal curl, lifting the head and shoulders, flexing the spine, and breathing out at the same time as the leg is lowered. Breathe in as the leg is returned and the head and shoulders are lowered and then repeat an abdominal curl as the other leg is moved out and lowered. NB: This is a very advanced progression and should be performed only by those with strong abdominals and a good conscious awareness of spinal stabilization or core stability.

Fig. 8.10   5. Advanced progression.

Kneeling Position to Contract the Lower Abdominals

This is a simple exercise, yet so important, involving those muscles responsible for core stability, the transverse abdominals.

- *Muscles targeted:* Transverse abdominis.
- *Technique:* Kneel in a 'box' position maintaining a neutral spine. Breathe out and at the same time slowly pull in the tummy by contracting the lower abdominals and without necessarily curving the spine. Hold that contraction and breathe normally for about seven to ten seconds. Then relax the contraction while slowly breathing out. Repeat about three or four times and perform regularly. Eventually, contraction of the lower abdominals should become instinctive and will form the basis of every exercise and every movement.
- *Safety tip:* Do not hold the breath. Try to breathe normally while holding the contraction.

Abdominal Exercises Not Recommended

Full Sit-ups with Straight Legs and Feet Anchored
- *Intended musculature:* Abdominals (rectus abdominis).

Fig. 8.11   *Starting position.*

Fig. 8.12   *Tummy pulled in.*

- *Primary muscles actually worked:* Hip flexors (ilio-psoas).
- *Secondary muscles involved:* Abdominals (rectus abdominis, transverse abdominis) attempt to stabilize the spine.
- *Potential dangers:* Straight legs and extended hips initially stretch the hip flexors, which pull the lumbar spine into hyper-extension.

Over-strengthening and shortening of the hip flexors, affecting posture and lumbar spine stability.

A high level of pulling force applied to the lumbar spine against a long lever.

If the hands are placed behind the head there may be a pulling force applied to the cervical (neck) vertebrae.

Figs 8.13a and b   Full sit-ups with straight legs and the feet anchored.

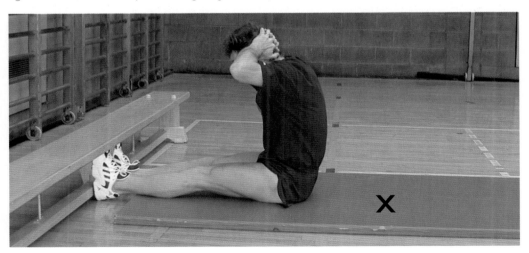

This exercise involves hip flexion, working the hip flexor muscles as prime movers. The exercise can exert excessive stress on the lower back and can shorten hip flexor muscles, leading to a hollow back and related postural problems. In addition, the hands are often clasped behind the head and tugging occurs which can place excessive stress on the cervical (neck) vertebrae.

Full Sit-ups with Twist on a Sloping Board

- *Intended musculature:* Obliques and abdominals.
- *Primary muscles actually worked:* Hip flexors (ilio-psoas) and obliques.
- *Secondary muscles involved:* Abdominals (rectus abdominis, transverse abdominis) attempt to stabilize the spine.
- *Potential dangers:* All the potential dangers associated with full sit-ups but still involves hip flexion and the associated pull on the lumbar spine.

Very high compressive force on the inter-vertebral discs plus rotation may elicit shear forces.

Very high level of pulling force applied to the lumbar spine against a long lever and against gravity.

Over-strengthening and shortening of the hip flexors, affecting posture and lumbar spine stability.

If the hands are placed behind the head there may be a pulling force applied to the cervical (neck) vertebrae.

This exercise has been traditionally practised to strengthen the obliques. However, the inter-vertebral discs are subjected to a very high compressive force and the twist can impose a shear force on those discs. I recommend twist curls performed on the floor.

Fig. 8.14   Full sit-ups with twist on a sloping board (potentially dangerous and not recommended). Very similar risks to the full sit-ups in Figs 8.13, but with the added risk of shear forces imposed on the inter-vertebral discs.

Piked Crunches

- *Intended musculature:* Abdominals (rectus abdominis, possibly lower fibres), lower abdominals (transverse abdominis).
- *Primary muscles actually worked:* Hip flexors (ilio-psoas).
- *Secondary muscles involved:* Abdominals (rectus abdominis, transverse abdominis) attempt to stabilize the spine.
- *Potential dangers:* Hip flexors are involved against a heavy resistance. Therefore there is a very high level of pulling force applied to the lumbar spine.

Fast, ballistic movement may elicit muscle strain.

Loss of balance and lack of stability may result in muscle strain.

This exercise can be hazardous. It involves fast ballistic movements, hip flexion, and the risk of loss of balance. Again, the hip flexors are employed against a long lever.

Straight-leg Raising

- *Intended musculature:* Abdominals (rectus abdominis, possibly lower fibres), lower abdominals (transverse abdominis).
- *Primary muscles actually worked:* Hip flexors (ilio-psoas).
- *Secondary muscles involved:* Abdominals (rectus abdominis, transverse abdominis) attempt to stabilize the spine.
- *Potential dangers:* Hip flexors are involved against a heavy resistance. Therefore there is a very high level of pulling force applied to the lumbar spine.

If the abdominals are not strong enough to stabilize the spine the lower back is pulled into hyper-extension, greatly increasing inter-vertebral disc pressure.

Fig. 8.15   Piked crunches (potentially dangerous and not recommended).

Very high intensity may cause holding of the breath. Very high internal (intra-abdominal) pressure is created.

A considerable increase in blood pressure if the position is held.

High risk of injury to the pelvic floor musculature, especially in females.

Straight-leg raising involves hip flexion and therefore the hip flexor muscles are worked against a very long and heavy lever. This exercise is considered to be dangerous and not recommended at all as very high stress is imposed on the lumbar spine with high pressure through the inter-vertebral discs.

This exercise has been traditionally performed as an abdominal strengthening exercise. It does involve the abdominal muscles in a stabilizing role (powerful isometric contractions), if the abdominal muscles are already strong enough to cope.

However, the major muscles being worked are the hip flexors that attach to the lumbar spine. These muscles contract very powerfully to lift the straight legs (flexion of the hip joints), which provide a very long resistance arm of the lever and therefore a very heavy resistance.

The hip flexors exert a very strong pull against their lumbar attachment and hyperextend the spine. If the abdominals are not strong enough they cannot hold down the lumbar spine. This results in hyper-extension of the lumbar spine, stretching of the abdominals which are trying to contract, extreme internal pressure in the abdominal cavity as the breath is held: a dangerous situation (Mitchell and Dale, 1980).

I have often heard it stated that leg raising works the lower abdominals, but what exactly do people mean by the *lower abdominals*? Rectus abdominis is one muscle extending from the lower ribs to the pubic bone of the pelvis. Although divided by bands of

Fig. 8.16   Straight-leg raising (potentially dangerous and not recommended).

connective tissue which are responsible for any 'rippling' effect when well developed, it is one sheet of muscle and does not consist of upper or lower muscles. It may be possible to place emphasis on upper or lower fibres, but leg-raising is not the way to achieve it safely.

Are the transverse abdominals considered to be the lower abdominals? If so, then straight leg-raising is not the answer either as this exercise can be potentially dangerous. A safer and more effective alternative is the reverse curl, discussed and illustrated previously.

Exercises for the Back

There are a number of exercises that help to strengthen the muscles that support and extend the spine. We need to develop

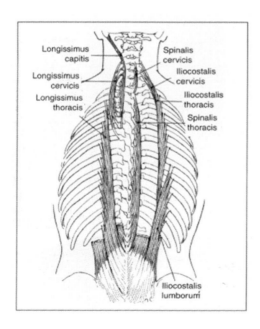

Fig. 8.17   The extensor muscles of the spine.

enough strength in these muscles to stabilize the spine and maintain good running posture.

Back Extensions
Back extensions are comparatively safe if performed correctly.

- Muscles worked: Extensors of the spine.
- Technique: Lying prone, keep the feet on the floor and slowly lift the upper body so that the chest rises a few centimetres from the floor. Breathe in while rising, pause momentarily, and breathe out while lowering.
- Safety tips: Do not lift the head too much, hyper-extending the neck. Breathe in time with the movement. Avoid fast, jerky, ballistic movements.

Back Extensions Slightly Modified
Even safer and very effective is a method of spinal extension derived from the Pilates method of body control. I have found this exercise to be far superior to any other, involving slow, controlled movement, working the spinal extensor muscles functionally and not through their inner range.

- *Muscles worked:* Extensors of the spine.
- *Technique:* Lie prone (face down) with the hands underneath the forehead. Pull in the tummy to stabilize the spine. Breathe in, and then as you exhale slowly tense the extensor muscles of the spine to lift the upper body so that the head and upper chest rise only a few centimetres from the floor. This occurs to a count of approximately four. Breathe in again and then lower as you exhale to a count of four. There is very little movement, yet adequate muscular tension is developed to elicit a strengthening and training effect.

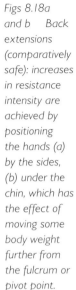

Figs 8.18a and b   Back extensions (comparatively safe): increases in resistance intensity are achieved by positioning the hands (a) by the sides, (b) under the chin, which has the effect of moving some body weight further from the fulcrum or pivot point.

- *Safety tip:* Think long, not high. Breathe in time with the movement.

Supine Pelvic Raising for the Extensors of the Spine and Hip, and for Lumbar Stability

Although with most toning exercises the muscles to be worked usually face upwards, the supine position for the start of this exercise dictates that the muscles of the back are facing downwards. However, contraction of those muscles raises the pelvis and spine from the floor. It is important that this exercise is carried out slowly and that breathing is compatible with the movement and vice versa.

- *Muscles worked:* Extensors of the spine, gluteals, transverse abdominis.
- *Technique:* Lying on your back, knees flexed and feet on the floor. Pull in the

Fig. 8.19a
Back
strengthening
and spinal
stabilization
exercise
according to
the Pilates
method:
relaxed
starting
position.

Fig. 8.19b
Raised position
(very little
movement).

tummy to stabilize the spine and tilt the pelvis (the pubis lifts). Breathe in but hold in the tummy. Then, while breathing out, as if lifting one vertebra at a time lift the pelvis, followed by the lower back so that eventually the upper back and shoulders are resting on the floor. Hold this position for a moment. Breathe in, and then as you breathe out slowly lower the back towards the floor, again, as if lowering one vertebra at a time. The tummy remains pulled in and the pelvis tilted until it is eventually lowered and rests on the floor.

- *Safety tip:* Work slowly. Breathe in time with the movement. Stabilize the lumbar spine by first of all pulling in the tummy (contracting transverse abdominis). Try to lift one vertebra at a time on the lift, and lower one at a time on the return.

Figs 8.20a, b, c, d, e, f and g   Supine pelvic raising to tone the muscles of the back and to develop lumbar stabilization.

Prone Supported Position for Trunk Stability (the Plank)

Holding this position involves isometric contraction of many muscles throughout the body, especially those around the trunk working as fixators to stabilize the spine.

- *Muscles worked:* Many muscles of the whole body working as fixators, but focusing on the transverse abdominals, consciously contracted to stabilize the lumbar spine.
- *Technique:* Lie prone with the elbows and forearms resting on the mat. Pull in the tummy by contracting the lower abdominals. Slowly exhale and at the same time lift the body into a forearm-supported position. Breathe normally and hold this position for about ten to twenty seconds, and then slowly lower to the resting position while breathing out.
- ***Safety tip:*** Be aware of maintaining a neutral spine throughout the supported position and do not let the hips sag. Do not hold the breath. Try to breathe normally throughout the held position. No need to perform the full position unless you are able – try the three-quarter position.

Fig. 8.21a   Starting position for the Plank.

Fig. 8.21b   Prone supported position for trunk stability.

Fig. 8.22a, b and c   Supine-lying trunk rotations.

Supine-lying Trunk Rotations for Spinal Mobility

- *Muscles worked:* The obliques, but also has a mobilizing effect on the spine.
- *Technique:* Lie on your back with the knees bent and feet flat on the floor. Have the arms out to the side on the floor like a 'crucifix'. Lower the knees in a controlled manner from side to side to rotate the spine. There is less momentum to take the spinal joints beyond their normal range and no body weight to produce a shearing force.
- *Safety tip:* Work slowly. Do not rush. Be in control. Do not force the position. Try to breathe normally and in time with the movement.

Supported Trunk Hyper-extensions with Hips Raised from the Floor

There has been considerable controversy concerning this exercise. In exercise teaching circles it has been considered potentially dangerous because the spine is suspended with the weight of the upper body pressing downwards. It is claimed that very high compressive forces are imposed upon the inter-vertebral discs and facet joints are forced together.

However, while discussing this exercise with a very well-qualified physiotherapist, I was told that this exercise is necessary, both to stretch the anterior ligaments of the spine and to reverse the anterior compression of the inter-vertebral discs. I now perform this exercise regularly.

The position is not necessarily held, but performed dynamically, raising and lowering with controlled movements.

If any doubt exists, a safer alternative is illustrated in Fig. 8.24. The upper body is supported on the forearms and the hips remain in contact with the floor.

Fig. 8.23 Supported trunk hyper-extensions with hips raised from the floor: controversial.

Fig. 8.24 Supported trunk extensions resting on the forearms.

Back Exercises *Not* Recommended

Standing Trunk Rotations with a Bar across the Shoulders (Potentially Dangerous)

This ballistic exercise is often performed to either strengthen the obliques or to mobilize the spine. However, it is potentially dangerous because the bar across the shoulders creates a momentum which rotates the spinal joints to the end of their range, thus tugging at the ligaments which stabilize those joints. In addition, the body weight is pressing down through the spinal column and rotation produces a shearing force in the inter-vertebral discs.

Ballistic Back Hyper-extensions

Do not lift both upper body and legs together into a ballistic hyper-extension. This compresses the inter-vertebral discs with high force and can also shorten the extensor muscles of the spine. It also forces together in a ballistic manner the facet joints of the spine, which can become inflamed.

Figs 8.25a and b   Ballistic trunk rotations with a bar across the shoulders (potentially dangerous and not recommended). Much safer is to perform supine-lying trunk rotations described previously in this chapter.

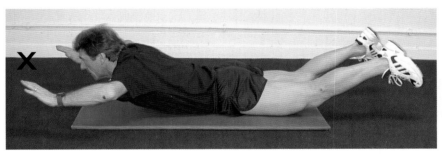

Fig. 8.26 Back hyper-extensions: potentially dangerous and not recommended.

CHAPTER 9

COMMON RUNNING INJURIES

No matter how careful we are, and despite all precautions and adherence to recommended practice, injuries may still occur. It can therefore be useful for the runner to have a working knowledge of some of the more common running injuries, self-treatment and rehabilitation.

NB: This section is not intended to be a substitute for the expert advice which can be offered by a fully qualified doctor or physiotherapist and such advice should be sought if any doubt or worry exists.

Categories of Injuries

Running injuries fall basically into two categories – **traumatic** and **overuse**.

Traumatic injuries occur suddenly and are usually instantly obvious. Such injuries usually occur as a result of sudden twisting, wrenching, over-stretching, collision or tripping and can include sudden immobilizing muscle tears, joint sprains, dislocations, contusions (bruising) and fractures.

Although some common symptoms may exist for many of the above-mentioned injuries, they may not always be obvious and a professional examination may be necessary to obtain an accurate diagnosis and advice on treatment and rehabilitation.

A bone fracture will usually be identified because of severe pain or tenderness over the site of the fracture, discolouration, swelling, deformity and immobility. However, all of these symptoms may not always be present and only an X-ray will show the fracture.

A twisted joint will usually be painful, may swell rapidly and may feel insecure. An accompanying fracture may be less obvious and, once again, only a qualified examination and an X-ray may reveal a fracture. Such a condition may occur with a severe sprain of the ankle where strong ligaments may pull away a piece of bone from the fibula of the lower leg (an avulsion fracture).

Certain hazards that exist increase the risk of traumatic injury – lamp posts to collide with, motor cars, cyclists, other pedestrians, pot holes, curb stones, tree roots. The advice here should be obvious – observe and concentrate and anticipate. Do not take risks.

Overuse injuries occur gradually over a period of time and if ignored may become severe and eventually result in immobilization. They are often caused by repetitive actions where incorrect bio-mechanics exist, too-rapid progression of training, inadequate rest/recovery to allow adaptation to occur, overtraining, or by excessive competition.

Overuse injuries can include gradually developing muscle and tendon strains, inflammatory or degenerative conditions of tendons and tendon sheaths and inflammation of joints.

Overuse of a tendon is referred to as a tendonopathy where there is degeneration of the tendon. Tenosynovitis is inflammation of the tendon sheath (the tendon should move freely within its surrounding sheath, lubricated by synovial fluid. Inflammation can cause adhesions where the tendon and sheath stick together); bursitis is an inflammation of a bursa (a fluid-filled sack near a joint to prevent friction where a tendon passes over bone).

Stages of Injury

Injuries can be **acute** or **chronic**.

The acute stage is when the injury has recently happened, usually within the first twenty-four to forty-eight hours. This is when first aid should be carried out aimed at reducing internal bleeding, swelling and inflammation.

Chronic injuries include those in which complications have developed, possibly because of incorrect treatment, lack of treatment, poor rehabilitation, returning to running before full healing and rehabilitation of the injury have occurred, or returning to training at too high an intensity. Chronic injuries can therefore be long-lasting or recurring.

Sprains and Strains

Possibly two of the most common types of running injuries are sprains and strains. These two very similar sounding words can sometimes be confused and misused.

Sprains are injuries to joints. They usually involve damage to the joint capsule, synovial membrane and ligaments (e.g. sprained ankle; twisted knee).

Strains are injuries to muscles and/or tendons and usually involve some degree of damage to the fibres. They are often known by distinctive names (e.g. a strained calf, a strained Achilles tendon; a 'pulled' hamstring). 'Pulled', torn, strained are all synonymous, although can sometimes refer to the degree of damage.

A muscle or tendon strain may be sudden (traumatic) or gradual (overuse). Although sometimes happening suddenly and with obvious consequences (a sprinter stops suddenly in a race clutching his/her hamstring), the sudden muscle tear may be the culmination of progressively occurring breakdown through overtraining, excessive training or racing. The injury is sudden and immobilizing (traumatic), but the cause may be overuse. Not too confusing really!

Grades or Degrees of Sprains and Strains

Joint Sprains

Grade 1: Minimal damage; some loss of function.

Grade 2: More ligament fibres damaged; partial detachment; some degree of instability; swelling.

Grade 3: Complete rupture; complete instability; swelling.

Muscle Strains

Grade 1: A small number of muscle fibres damaged; fascia intact (fascia is the very thin connective tissue which binds and encapsulates the muscle and muscle fibres); minimal bleeding.

Grade 2: A larger number of muscle fibres damaged; fascia intact; considerable bleeding which can be felt as 'mass' (if bleeding heals as a lump, it becomes an intra-muscular haematoma).

Grade 3: A much larger number of muscle fibres damaged; fascia torn; bleeding diffuses and fills tissue spaces; inter-muscular haematoma (blood seeps between muscles and can be seen as bruise-like discolouration).

Grade 4: Complete rupture of the muscle; a gap can be felt between the two ends.

Soft Tissue Injuries

Soft tissue includes muscle, tendon, ligament, synovial membrane, tendon sheath and skin. **Hard tissue** includes bone and cartilage.

Soft tissue injuries usually result from contact (bruising), twisting and over-stressing joints (sprains), rapid over-stretching of muscles or tendons (traumatic strains), chafing and rubbing (local inflammation), fatigue and excessive repetitive action (overuse strains).

Inflammation is the body's reaction to injury or irritation. Typical symptoms involve local heat, pain, redness, swelling, although not all symptoms may be present.

Inflammation can occur at a muscle's tendonous attachment to a bone. To be precise, tendons attach to the periostium, the very thin fascia which surrounds the bone. Inflammation here is known as tenoperiostitis. One common overuse running injury known as medial tibial stress syndrome (one cause of shin pain, to which runners give the global term 'shin splints') is a form of tenoperiostitis (inflammation caused

by microscopic damage to the tendon and its attachment to the periostium of the tibia) and may be described as 'the tendon pulling away from the bone'. Other running injury examples of tenoperiostitis include groin strain (where the adductor muscles of the inner thigh attach to the pubic bone of the pelvis, and plantar fasciitis under the heel of the foot where the plantar fascia attaches to the calcaneus (heel bone).

Anti-inflammatory creams and gels can be obtained from the pharmacy and can be effective in reducing inflammation if used regularly as directed. Patience may be required with inflammation as it can be difficult and persistent.

Treatment of Soft Tissue Injuries

Immediate first-aid treatment of soft tissue injuries is concerned with controlling inflammation, internal bleeding and swelling, thus alleviating pain to some degree and promoting faster healing and reducing the likelihood of complications.

Immediate first-aid treatment of soft tissue injuries involves **R.I.C.E. – Rest, Ice, Compression, Elevation**.

Rest may be immediately obvious or inevitable as sudden pain, pain on attempted movement, fear of further damage and swelling may prevent movement. However, a longer period of rest will be required to allow the damaged tissue to start healing. This period of rest will vary according to the severity of the injury; it could be a few days or one or two weeks. Rest of the injured body part may involve complete rest and abstention from any attempt to run, but once healing is in progress, 'active' rest may involve gentle movements of the joint or muscle concerned.

Unfortunately, rest is something that runners are not very good at and they often return to the activity too soon. For a runner, two weeks with no running is a very long time, but discipline is required, for two weeks' rest can prevent many more weeks of despair.

Ice should be applied to the injured part as soon as possible. It may be ice in a polythene bag or an ice-cold gel pack from the freezer. It should not be placed directly on to the skin. A towel or other piece of material should be placed between the cold compress and the skin to prevent an ice 'burn'. A bag of frozen peas can be a handy first-aid item to have in the freezer as it will mould to the shape of the body part (but mark the packet and be sure not to use it for food). Ice should be applied for about ten to fifteen minutes, but should not be reapplied within an hour. It needs to be applied regularly, daily for the first few days (acute stage) and may be beneficial used regularly over a period of time.

Physiological effects of ice treatment:
- Reduces pain by reducing conductivity of nerve fibres.
- Reduces stiffness. Spasm is a natural reaction to pain. By reducing pain, ice reduces spasm.
- Reduces swelling. The initial response of the tissue is vasoconstriction (closing down of blood vessels). This limits the flow of blood and the swelling (oedema).
- Promotes repair. After the initial response of vasoconstriction, if ice remains applied there follows vasodilatation (opening up of blood vessels which increases blood flow to help repair the damaged tissue). Longer applications of ice (about twenty minutes) may be applied later, during the healing stage of the injury.

Compression in the form of an elasticated bandage will help to control the swelling. Swelling is not a bad thing initially; it is the body's

> Do not apply heat during the acute stage of a soft tissue injury. Heat will stimulate bleeding and inflammation.

natural 'splinting' mechanism which prevents further damage to an injured part by restricting movement. However, the body tends to over-compensate and swelling may be excessive, causing pressure, pain and discomfort. Excess swelling can hinder the healing process and lead to complications, or may prevent an early diagnosis by a qualified person. Swelling is caused by fluid in the inter-cellular spaces and is known as oedema. Oedema differs from normal tissue fluid in that it contains plasma proteins and fibrinogen, a substance which causes blood to clot. Oedema is a viscous fluid which can become more viscous (sticky) and adhesions can then occur. Tissues which should normally slide smoothly over each other become stuck together. Controlling the swelling by ice, compression and elevation, and later by gentle movement, can help prevent the formation of adhesions.

Elevation also helps to control the swelling because fluids naturally flow downwards with gravity. Raising (elevating) the injured part will help drain the oedema, reducing pressure and discomfort.

Acute oedema forms the swelling during the acute stage of an injury. It is the acute oedema that we try to control with R.I.C.E. treatment. Acute oedema will be soft, puffy, painful and will pit readily on pressure.

Chronic oedema can form if swelling is not controlled during the acute stage. Chronic oedema is then difficult to disperse and may require much massaging and frictions to break down adhesions. Chronic oedema is tense and harder, and the skin may be shiny; there is little pitting on pressure.

Massage may be of benefit in the rehabilitation of soft tissue injuries, particularly muscle strains and joint sprains, *but only when healing is well underway.* Do not attempt self hands-on massage, or let anybody else apply hands-on massage during the acute stage. If massage is to be considered, it should be performed by a very well-qualified and knowledgeable practitioner, and preferably by a qualified physiotherapist who may also employ electrotherapy.

Rehabilitation of Joint Injuries

As soon as possible after injury, and after a period of healing has taken place, very gentle joint movement may take place. This may be in the form of passive movement (another person, preferably qualified and experienced moves the joint through its range), or may be active (where the injured person moves the joint).

Movement for an injured joint during the rehabilitation stage acts as a form of natural massage and helps to reduce swelling. It helps to lubricate the joint by stimulating the secretion of synovial fluid. In addition, it helps to maintain some degree of tone, strength and suppleness in the muscles that influence the joint. All remedial movements of an injured joint should be carried out within the limits of pain.

Rehabilitation of Muscles and Tendons

Injury to a muscle or tendon will heal better if the muscle is gently stretched as soon as possible after the acute stage. On healing, scar tissue forms. Gentle stretching helps the scar tissue to form long and even, in the direction of the muscle/tendon fibres and not tight

and irregular. Gentle movement also encourages blood flow to bring healing nutrients and helps to maintain some strength, tone and suppleness.

Scar tissue can contract a few weeks after its formation and can continue to contract if allowed to. It is therefore necessary to stretch the scar tissue while it is being laid down after the acute stage has passed. This stretching should be continued regularly for several months after the injury; in fact stretching of all running muscles should be an integral part of any training programme.

The Use of Heat During Rehabilitation

As previously mentioned, heat should not be used during the acute stage of a soft tissue injury. After the acute stage (which can vary according to the severity of the injury), heat can be beneficial to the healing process. Heat can be applied by using a (warm) hot water bottle, heated gel pack or infra-red heat lamp. Do not position the lamp too close to the skin. Heat encourages blood flow (vasodilatation) to the affected area, which supplies nutrients and healing substances, increases muscle metabolism and increases muscle relaxation.

An Explanation of Some Common Running-related Injuries and Conditions

Metatarsalgia

Pain is felt in the fore-foot, under the metatarsal heads, where the toes meet the foot proper. It is often the result of excessive impact involving that part of the foot and can occur in persons new to running, possibly because of too rapid a progression (too much too soon), or with established runners who might increase their mileage excessively.

The application of ice can help reduce inflammation and pain, but rest from the causative activity is essential for a while. Foot exercises can help mobilize the joints and strengthen the muscles of the foot, improving the arches.

Plantar Fasciitis

Pain is felt on the underside of the foot towards the heel and may feel as if there is a small stone in the shoe at that point. The plantar fascia is a strip of connective tissue on the underside of the foot connecting the heads of the middle three metatarsal bones near the toes to the calcaneus (heel bone). It is at the attachment to the heel bone where inflammation can develop.

Causes may include an increase in mileage or some other change which stretches the underside of the foot.

Initial treatment may involve applying ice at the painful site on the underside of the heel and an arch support might help. A consultation with a qualified medical practitioner or physiotherapist would be recommended. If not treated properly, this condition can become chronic, resulting in considerable pain, not only when running (which should not be performed), but also when walking and standing.

Spring Ligament Strain

Though less common than plantar fasciitis, spring ligament strain is very similar, although pain is felt towards the inner of the underside of the foot near the heel. Again, the application of ice and an arch support may help and a professional diagnosis should be sought.

Athletes' Foot

Athletes' foot is a fungal infection of the skin on the feet. It can occur anywhere on the foot, but is most common between the toes. It is an infectious condition which can be spread from one person to another through contact with floors, or can be spread from one foot to the other by transferring unclean socks.

The condition causes itching and can become painful. The skin can appear white and moist, especially between the toes. Similar fungal conditions around the rest of the foot may result in dry, flaky skin which cracks and becomes sore.

It can be fairly common with runners as they are often (a) barefoot in changing rooms and showers, and (b) they generate inside their running shoes warm, moist conditions ideal for the fungus to thrive.

Its development can be reduced by good foot hygiene. Feet should be washed regularly, preferably after every run and should be thoroughly dried, particularly between the toes. The application of anti-fungal powder may help prevent it and it is advisable to wear flip-flops in communal showers and changing rooms.

If the condition does occur, it is simple to treat with any of the many athletes' foot treatment creams and liquids commercially available. Less expensive, and it works, is the application of lemon juice. Treatment should be continued for a while after the condition appears to have cleared up.

Verruca

A verruca is an in-growing wart (plantar wart), found on the underside of the foot. It is caused by a virus and can be spread by barefoot contact with floors, or from one foot to the other by interchanging infected socks.

In the early stages, a verruca appears as a small black spot. If untreated and allowed to develop, it can enlarge and may appear like a small volcano-like crater. At this stage it will be painful to walk or stand on.

Treatment is with a verruca medication which contains salicylic acid. Correct strengths should be obtained with advice from a doctor, chiropodist or podiatrist.

Sprained Ankle

A sprained ankle is one of the most common running injuries and the most common type of ankle sprain is an **inversion sprain**, where the person 'goes over' on the ankle, the weight going over the outside of the ankle, turning the foot inwards.

Damage occurs to the lateral ligaments which hold the joint firm on the outside. Immediate treatment is R.I.C.E. (rest, ice, compression, elevation). As soon as possible (preferably immediately, but not usually possible when out running) ice should be applied. Compression in the form of an elasticated bandage should be applied. This should cover an extensive area from the toes to just below the knee, otherwise swelling can occur at the edges of the compressive bandage. The injured ankle should be raised whenever possible to a level higher than the hip to allow fluid to drain away.

With a severe ankle sprain a hospital check should be carried out which may involve an X-ray as there is the possibility that a fracture has occurred, usually at the lower end of the fibula, to which the lateral ligaments are attached. There could be an avulsion fracture, where the strong ligament pulls away pieces of bone.

Other types of ankle sprain can occur. The foot may be forced outwards with the body weight over the inner edge. This may be accompanied by damage to the medial (inner) aspect of the knee joint. The foot may be forced upwards (dorsi-flexion) or downwards (plantar-flexion). Whatever type of sprain, the initial treatment is R.I.C.E. and medical attention is recommended.

Rehabilitation: With an ankle sprain, a short period of immobilization may be required during the acute stage. During this stage, ice should be applied regularly for about ten minutes and the foot elevated. After approximately forty-eight hours (but depending on the severity) ice may be applied for longer. Rest from strenuous weight-bearing activity is essential, so no running for a while. Elevation may still be necessary for some time to control persistent swelling.

To regain some muscle strength, isometric exercises (muscle tension without joint movement) can be carried out. While sitting with the feet on the floor, press the toes/forefoot down against the floor working the calf muscles at the back of the lower leg. If the uninjured foot is placed on top of the injured foot, the lower foot can be tilted upwards (pivoting from the heel) to work the anterior tibial muscles at the front of the lower leg.

Gentle stretching should be performed, within the limits of pain, as soon as possible during the healing stage. Stretching allows the scar tissue to form in neat, long layers, in the direction of the ligament fibres.

Stretching will involve gently turning the foot inwards (inversion – the same direction that caused the injury, but now slowly, controlled and within the limits of pain). Eventually, body weight can be applied to the stretch.

When weight bearing is possible, balancing on one leg or use of a wobble board can develop strength and proprioception in the muscles of the lower leg, which will have weakened during the period of immobilization and rest.

Calf Strain

The calf is the region at the back of the lower leg. As well as three deep posterior tibial muscles, the main calf muscles are gastrocnemius (superficial) and soleus (deeper). Both insert to the back of the heel bone via the Achilles tendon at the lower end; soleus attaches to the tibia and fibula at the upper end (origin) and gastrocnemius crosses the back of the knee joint and attaches to the back lower end of the femur.

Gastrocnemius is more commonly the muscle damaged and pain may be felt in the belly of the muscle or at its junction with the Achilles tendon. Running should cease immediately pain is felt or further damage will occur. There may a hint of pain which increases over a period of time, or there may be a sudden sharp pain which stops the activity.

Immediate treatment is ice and rest. Ongoing treatment during the acute (painful) stage will include rest, ice, compression and elevation. Rest from running may be up to two weeks to allow full healing to take place.

As soon as possible after the acute stage, gentle stretching can be carried out keeping well within the limits of pain. This encourages scar tissue to form evenly and longitudinally.

Rehabilitation: Regular calf stretching is important during rehabilitation, along with simple strengthening exercises (calf raises – up onto the toes). When returning to functional activity, a period of walking should take place before attempting to run. When running is commenced again, it should be slow and short for a couple of sessions. You will be back down the fitness ladder and should not expect to return immediately to running at the pre-injury level.

Achilles Tendon Strain

As with the calf, an Achilles tendon strain can occur suddenly or could develop gradually with a hint of pain occurring during a number of runs. Sudden pain will cause the runner to stop, but gradual pain is a sign that a more serious strain is developing and treatment should begin at that stage in the form of rest and ice application. Unfortunately, runners find it very difficult to rest when the condition does not actually stop them, but common sense and discipline is required as the condition can become chronic if not treated properly.

In severe cases rest from running may be at least six weeks and could be up to six months. Many runners return to running too soon and then complain when pain returns or persists.

Deep friction massage over the damaged spot can help break down adhesions, but this should be carried out by a qualified person or under the direction of a phy-siotherapist.

Rehabilitation: As with a calf strain, gentle stretching and strengthening should be carried out before returning to functional activities, which will include walking initially. Running should only be resumed once the person can hop without pain, and then should be slow and short for a while.

Eccentric exercises (lengthening whilst under load) should be undertaken, following advice from a physiotherapist, with eccentric loading being helpful for most tendon injuries, although the mechanism of this benefit is unknown.

Shin Splints

Shin splints can be an umbrella term which describes pain felt along the inner or outer edge of the shin bone (tibia) at the front of the lower leg. A qualified diagnosis should be sought as the pain could result from any of a number of causes:

- Strain of the anterior tibial muscle on the outer side of the shin.
- Strain of the posterior tibial muscle behind the shin bone.
- Compartment syndrome – a lower leg muscle may swell during activity and

stretches its comparatively inelastic containing sheath.
- True shin splints – microscopic damage to fibres where the muscle attaches to the shin bone with resulting inflammation.
- Rarely a stress fracture.

Any of the above-mentioned conditions can be brought about by the repeated high impact of running, but usually because of excesses such as too rapid progression or a sudden increase in mileage.

Treatment involves rest and ice (along the painful area of the shin). Physiotherapy is recommended and attention to the precipitating cause.

Runner's Knee

Like 'shin splints', runner's knee is not a condition in itself, but a term applied to a number of painful conditions affecting the knee joint:

Knee Cap Pain

Pain is felt across the lower edge of the knee cap (patella), possibly along the sides of the knee cap, especially when going up or down stairs/steps or when running up or down hills. It may also be referred to as patello-femoral pain as the cause is often a fault in the tracking of the knee cap where it articulates with the lower end of the thigh bone (femur), causing the knee cap to rub against the side of the groove in the head of the femur instead of sliding smoothly when the knee is flexed and extended.

This may rarely in its most severe form result in **chondromalacia patella** – a degeneration of the cartilage lining the under surface of the knee cap, but fortunately these changes in the cartilage may never occur. The tracking fault may be caused by a reduction in strength of the inner quadriceps muscle (vastus medialis). All four quadriceps muscles attach to the tibia below the knee joint via the quadriceps (or patellar) tendon. When the strength of all four quadriceps muscles are in balance, the knee cap is correctly aligned in its femoral groove, but if vastus medialis weakens the outer three muscles (particularly vastus lateralis)

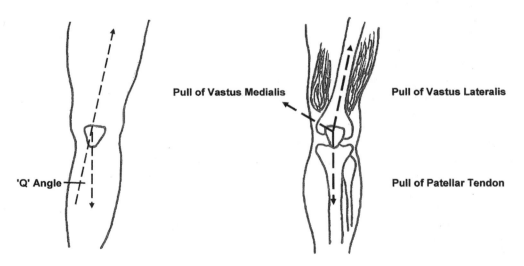

Pull of Vastus Medialis

Pull of Vastus Lateralis

'Q' Angle

Pull of Patellar Tendon

Fig. 9.1   The knee cap held in place by the quadriceps muscles and the patellar tendon.

pull the knee cap laterally out of alignment (see Fig. 9.1).

Treatment and rehabilitation can simply involve strengthening the vastus medialis muscle to re-align the knee cap. To specifically work vastus medialis, tension must be developed in the muscle with the knee straight (extended). See Figs 9.2, 9.3 and 9.4.

Knee cap/patello-femoral pain can occasionally be attributed to an excessive 'Q' angle at the knee (angle between the thigh bone [femur] and the shin bone [tibia]) because of a wider pelvis and so, as a possible contributory factor, may be more common in females). (See Fig. 9.5.)

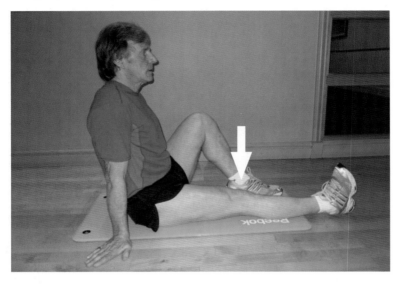

Fig. 9.2   1. Sitting on the floor with one leg out straight; press the back of the knee down against the floor.

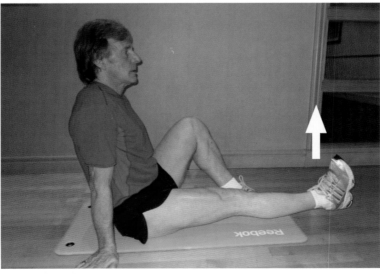

Fig. 9.3   2. Sitting on the floor with one leg out straight; lift the straight leg up (raise the heel from the floor) a short distance, lower, then repeat the action ten times.

Figs 9.4a and b   3. As above, but with a rolled-up towel under the back of the knee. Contract the quadriceps, which will extend the knee fully and lift the heel off the floor.

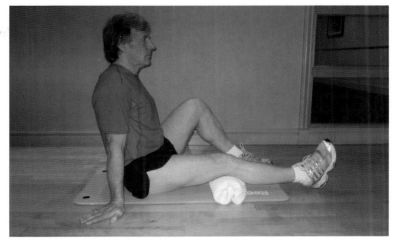

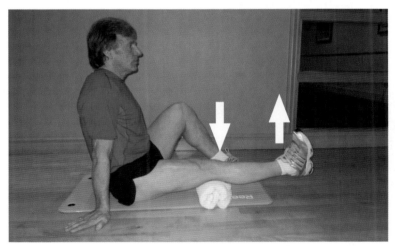

liotibial Band Syndrome (IBS)

This is a common overuse condition with runners. Pain is felt on the outer side of the knee. The pain may appear some way into a run and gradually increase to the point where it stops the activity.

The pain is the result of irritation of the iliotibial band, a band of fascia (strong, thin

> Quadriceps strengthening on a gymnasium leg extension machine is not recommended as the dynamic movement of the knee cap under tension can aggravate the condition. Also not recommended is the wearing of a knee bandage/support without a knee cap hole as it will force the knee cap down against the femur.

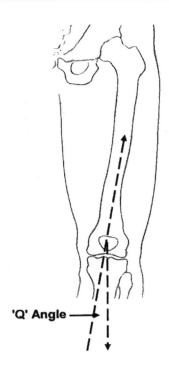

Fig. 9.5 The 'Q' angle is the angle between the femur and the tibia.

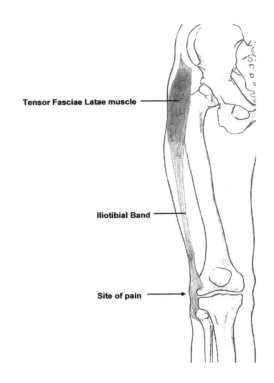

Fig. 9.6 Tensor fasciae latae muscle and the iliotibial band.

tissue) connecting the gluteal muscles and the muscle on the upper/outer side of the hip/thigh (tensor fasciae latae) to the tibia below the knee. Therefore it passes over the side of the knee joint. During repetitive actions such as running, the iliotibial band moves to and fro across the side of the knee joint and can cause irritation. One cause can be tension in the tensor fasciae latae, which transmits tension through the iliotibial band. (See Fig. 9.6.)

Treatment involves the application of ice for ten minutes over the site of pain and rest from running. Stretching of the tensor fasciae latae muscle and gluteal muscles will help to reduce the tension (see Chapter 3).

Quadriceps Strain

The quadriceps, as powerful extensors of the knee, will be heavily taxed, especially on downhill running where powerful eccentric contraction is required. As rectus femoris crosses both the knee joint and the hip joint, this particular muscle in the quadriceps group can be more prone to damage (as can all muscles crossing two joints).

Like any muscle strain, rest and ice form the main initial treatment and should be continued for a considerable length of time. Heat should not be applied during the acute stage. As healing is taking place, well after the acute stage, heat may be applied to encourage blood and nutrients to the muscle. Gentle quadriceps stretching during healing can help elongate scar tissue. Rest from any activity which causes pain; this may require discipline. Many runners try to return too soon.

Massage is not recommended with a severe quadriceps strain as hands-on manipulation can cause complications in the form of tiny bone formations (deposits of calcium) within the fibres, known as myositis ossificans.

Rehabilitation may involve progressive quadriceps strengthening exercises and walking before returning to running. You will have moved way down the fitness ladder and so the initial runs need to be short and gentle; increase in achievable progressions. Stretching is important during rehabilitation, as it should be on a regular basis when fit.

Hamstring Strain

The hamstrings, crossing two joints, are also vulnerable, and often hamstring damage can be attributed to either an imbalance of strengths between quadriceps and hamstrings, or a lack of flexibility.

For a hamstring strain, almost the same advice could be given as with a quadriceps strain – rest, ice, compression and elevation. *Heat should not be applied* during the acute stage, but can be beneficial well into the healing and rehabilitation stage. Hamstrings can respond to skilled massage during rehabilitation and gentle stretching is recommended. **Rehabilitation** can involve progressive strengthening and stretching and walking before returning to gentle running.

Groin Strain

A delicate area to apply ice, but ice is necessary to reduce inflammation to the adductor tendon. Rest should be obvious and stretching of the adductor muscles can help reduce tension at the tendonous attachment.

Pain in the groin may be a symptom of another condition such as an inguinal hernia, inflammation of the inguinal ligament or pubic symphysis, or may be referred pain from the back. If pain persists, it is recommended that an expert diagnosis should be obtained.

Metatarsal Stress Fracture

Stress fractures can occur in the metatarsal bones, with fairly acute pain felt in the forefoot. The cause is usually repeated heavy loading through an excessive increase in mileage or too high intensity after a lay-off. The condition commonly occurs in the second metatarsal and is known as a **march fracture** as it became common with soldiers marching considerable distances in ill-fitting boots.

Pain along the outer side of the foot could be a stress fracture of the fifth metatarsal along its shaft. An expert diagnosis should be obtained and if a stress fracture is confirmed, then a long period of rest is essential (possibly up to six weeks).

When eventually returning to running, it must be remembered that you will be way down the fitness ladder and it is vital that a very gentle come-back is performed. This might involve a week or two of regular walking before progressing to short, easy runs.

With all overuse/chronic injuries it is important to consider causes so that these can be remedied to avoid recurrence.

CHAPTER 10

DIET AND INJURY PREVENTION

The quality of one's diet does not only influence general, everyday health and well-being; for runners the quality of diet may contribute towards the prevention of injury.

The main dietary food substances are **protein**, **fat** and **carbohydrate**, along with **water**. Together they provide all the other essential nutrients such as vitamins, minerals and fibre.

It is important that all the main food substances are eaten in the correct proportions. Most people in the Western developed world are not short of food. There is food in abundance and people are able to eat on a regular basis every day. They are not under-nourished, but many are malnourished. Although they are getting plenty of food, it may be heavily processed with an excess of certain food substances at the expense of others.

For example, much processed food is high in fat, and particularly in saturated fat. The diet might be overloaded in fat and too low in carbohydrate and, therefore, fibre. Also, protein can often be particularly tasty, and emphasis may be on meat with neglect for carbohydrate.

Protein is vitally important in a runner's diet for the repair and rebuilding of damaged muscle (catabolism during training; anabolism and adaptation during rest), but only in recommended amounts. Excesses of protein will be stored as fat.

Fat is also important in a runner's diet, but only the recommended amount. Although fat becomes the main energy 'fuel' during lower intensity, longer runs, it can only be metabolized if there is adequate carbohydrate present. If runners 'hit the wall' in a marathon, it is because they have exhausted their supply of muscle glycogen and the body struggles to burn fat as fuel. In addition, there is enough fat stored in the body to provide survival energy for weeks if a condition of starvation existed.

Recommended Amounts

There are many different terms used concerning recommended amounts of calories and food substances. We risk being confused by Dietary Reference Values (DRV), Recommended Nutrient Intakes (RNI), Recommended Daily Allowances (RDA), Estimated Average Requirements (EAR) and Reference Nutritional Intake (RNI).

In 1991 the Department of Health published new Dietary Reference Values (DRV) to replace the 1979 Recommended Daily Allowances (RDA). It can be very confusing, but let's try to keep it simple.

I prefer to use the term 'recommended amounts'. The International Conference on Foods, Nutrition and Performance (1991), along with the World Health Organization (WHO), recommended the following daily amounts of the various food substances to maintain a healthy state in the body: **protein 10–15 per cent, fat 15–30 per cent,** carbohydrate **60–70 per cent**. There is a range for each food substance and amounts of each may vary according to lifestyle and activity level.

Water should be consumed on a regular basis throughout the day, and, with the recommended proportions of food substances, adequate amounts of vitamins, minerals and fibre should be obtained. Unfortunately, in affluent countries many people consume over 40 per cent of their daily calories from fat (Bean, 1996). This has to be at the expense of carbohydrate.

Although all three food substances are important in a healthy diet, and protein and fat have been very briefly discussed, this chapter focuses on the importance of carbohydrate in the runner's diet and also the importance of fluid intake during training and competition.

Carbohydrate

Carbohydrate is the true energy food and should form the bulk of an active person's diet. All carbohydrate is broken down during digestion to its simplest form, glucose, which can then be absorbed into the blood stream and used immediately for energy, or converted to glycogen, a glucose polymer, and stored in the muscles and liver.

Liver glycogen is mainly responsible for supplying the brain with glucose for nervous energy and levels can fall considerably overnight. For this reason breakfast is a vitally important meal for active people. Muscle glycogen can be deployed for physical work energy and levels are maintained by a high percentage of carbohydrate in the diet.

Although providing fewer calories per gram (four) than fat (nine), carbohydrate is the most accessible fuel for muscular energy.

Even working aerobically at low to moderate intensities, although fat will be the major fuel for energy, it cannot be metabolized unless there is carbohydrate present.

There are two types of carbohydrate, **complex carbohydrate** (starches) and **simple carbohydrate** (sugars). Complex carbohydrate is the bulky type of carbohydrate obtained from potatoes, pasta, rice, bread and other vegetable sources, and is often very rich in other nutrients. Simple carbohydrate is in the form of sugar, glucose powder and glucose syrup. It provides little nutritional value except pure energy, often lacking other nutrients.

Complex carbohydrate should form the bulk of an active person's diet as it provides the major source of energy, along with many other nutrients, for an active lifestyle. However, simple carbohydrate can also be of value to the athlete as it is a source of carbohydrate to replete or maintain muscle glycogen stores.

Simple carbohydrate can also be of value *during* long endurance events of over three hours' duration as it is quickly digested, absorbed, and can be used to provide energy when glycogen stores in the muscles are getting low. In events lasting two to three hours there should be sufficient glycogen stored in the muscles for the duration of the event, especially if the athlete has consumed a regular high carbohydrate diet and has carbohydrate loaded prior to the event. Also the athlete should have trained properly (adequate long slow distance) to make the body more efficient at metabolizing fat as fuel for energy, thus conserving glycogen supplies in the muscles.

Muscle glycogen depletion can contribute towards the breakdown of muscle tissue. Muscle fibres are made up of muscle filaments, which in turn are made up of the protein filaments, actin and myosin. If muscle glycogen stores become severely depleted, it is difficult for the body to metabolize fat for energy and muscle protein becomes an emergency energy supply. We are literally breaking down the muscles employed during running. The result may be severe muscle fatigue.

It has been recommended traditionally that the carbohydrate intake of physically active people should consist mainly of *complex* carbohydrate such as potatoes, pasta, bread and rice as it is digested and absorbed much more slowly and therefore its energy release is more sustained and longer-lasting. Simple carbohydrates such as sugar, glucose, sucrose, maltose and fructose, which are quickly digested and absorbed, cause a short-term rapid rise in blood glucose, with a corresponding increase in insulin (a hormone whose action lowers the blood glucose level) secretion. This in turn results in a rapid reduction in blood glucose. However, the categorizing of carbohydrates into simple and complex, and the fact that simple carbohydrates invoke a faster glucose/insulin response if consumed during periods of inactivity, is an over-simplification.

Actually, certain carbohydrate foods from both groups can be quickly digested and absorbed, resulting in a rapid glucose/insulin response. Some complex carbohydrates such as potatoes, white bread and white rice are digested and absorbed quickly and have a **high glycaemic index**. The simple carbohydrate fructose, found in fruit, is digested and absorbed slowly and has a **low glycaemic index** (Carlton, 2001; Bean, 1996, 1999; Brand-Miller, 1998).

Fig. 10.1 Glycaemic index of a number of carbohydrate foods popular with physically active people (sources: Bean, 1996, 1999; Brand-Miller, 1998).

High GI (60–100)		Moderate GI (40–60)		Low GI (<40)	
Food	**GI**	**Food**	**GI**	**Food**	**GI**
White bread	69	Wholemeal pasta	42	Apple	36
Wholemeal bread	72	White pasta	50	Grapefruit	26
Brown rice	80	Spaghetti	41	Chickpeas	33
White rice	82	Oatmeal biscuits	55	Lentils	28
Potatoes	85 (av)	Porridge	50	Peach (fresh)	28
Bananas	60	Carrots	49	Yoghurt (low fat)	36
Raisins	64	Sweet corn	53 (av)	Skimmed milk	32
Muesli	66	Baked beans	48		
Cornflakes	77	Grapes	43		
Weetabix	75	Orange	43		
Shredded Wheat	67	Honey	58		

Glycaemic Index (GI)

The Glycaemic Index (GI), introduced in the early 1980s, is a system used to classify carbohydrate foods according to the extent to which they raise blood glucose levels after consumption. The GI of a food is calculated by comparing the blood glucose level after consuming 50g of a particular type of carbohydrate against that following ingestion of 50g of pure glucose, the glucose itself having a GI of 100 (graphically expressed as a curve, showing amount over a certain time) (Carlton, 2001; Bean, 1996, 1999).

This knowledge is of importance to runners who may need to quickly replenish carbohydrate (glycogen) stores in the body, or may need to maintain adequate glycogen stores for regular physical activity. Quick replenishment of glycogen may require immedi-

> The glycaemic index of carbohydrate is influenced by the presence of other food substances consumed at the same time. It is also influenced by the presence of combined fibre, fat and protein, and by cooking.

ate ingestion of high GI carbohydrate foods very soon after a competitive event or long run, followed by frequent consumption of high GI carbohydrates over a 24-hour period.

However, long-term, a mix of both complex and simple carbohydrates and a combination of high, moderate and low GI carbohydrates should be consumed, not only for the carbohydrate itself, but also for the additional nutrients that many complex carbohydrates contain. In addition, although carbohydrate may be the prime 'fuel' for athletes and active people, adequate protein and fat should form a vital part of the healthy, balanced diet.

Carbohydrate Loading

Carbohydrate loading is often used by endurance athletes prior to a long competitive event (marathon, triathlon, etc.) to achieve maximal glycogen stores in the muscles at the beginning of the event. The traditional 'deplete and load' method is no longer advised and therefore not discussed here. It has been superseded by the 'taper and load' method.

Taper and Load

Instead of a very hard training session to deplete the glycogen stores, it may be desirable to continue normal training up to a week before the event while consuming the athlete's normal high carbohydrate diet.

In the final week training is tapered down during the first three days, but normal high carbohydrate is still consumed. For the final three days the athlete rests and also attempts to consume even higher quantities of carbohydrate.

This method is safer because the athlete can judge higher than usual quantities of carbohydrate. All that is required is to increase what is normally consumed. However, again it is bulky food and so it may be convenient to use carbohydrate powder mixed with water to be taken as a drink. This will also help to maintain fluid levels. (Runners should appreciate that fluid is retained with CBH, so should not be concerned with this producing weight gain; it has the advantage that for a long run/race there is already 'extra' fluid on board, becoming available as the CBH/glycogen is utilized.)

Fig. 10.2   Taper and carbohydrate load

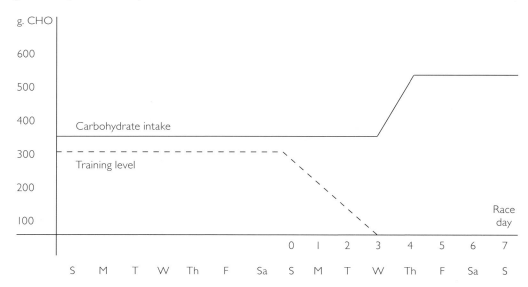

After a long run it is important to consume carbohydrate as soon as possible and ideally within two hours. Delaying carbohydrate intake for a couple of hours after exercise reduces the rate of glycogen resynthesis. At least one gram of carbohydrate per kilogram of body weight (1g/kg) is recommended, and this may be in the form of a carbohydrate drink, energy bars, bananas, or other solid foods if they can be tolerated so soon after the end of the event. The carbohydrate drink will also assist with re-hydration. High carbohydrate intake should continue for about twenty-four hours.

Water/Fluid Intake

The body consists of 50–60 per cent water. Water is within every single cell (intra-cellular) and around every cell (extra-cellular). The plasma of the blood is water, which carries many dissolved particles, and water forms the intestinal juices and lymph.

Muscle is 75 per cent water, whereas fat is less than 25 per cent water. Therefore a person with a reduced percentage body fat and more lean tissue should contain more water than a person with a higher percentage body fat and less lean tissue.

We may survive for quite a while without food, but would not survive very long without water. Intake of water is vital when running, both during training and in competition, particularly in warm or hot conditions. A 2 per cent dehydration can result in up to a 20 per cent reduction in performance. So it is vital that the marathon runner consumes water regularly during the event.

Dehydration impairs performance during prolonged periods of physical activity and so fluid intake must be part of nutritional strategies for competition and training (Williams, 1995).

Dehydration lowers performance by reducing blood volume, cardiac output (amount of blood pumped by the heart per minute) and the speed of blood flow. With a reduction in circulating blood flow, a circulatory deficiency results, causing an increase in heart rate. In addition it can result in difficulty in breathing, gastro-intestinal upsets, nausea, lack of appetite and difficulty in muscular movements.

If blood volume is significantly reduced through dehydration, endurance performance and temperature regulation are impaired. Performance decrements have been noted following dehydration of 2 per cent bodyweight. At greater levels of dehydration there are dramatic declines in endurance performance and elevations in heart rate and core body temperature (Pyke and Sutton, 1992).

When water is lost from the body, blood plasma has a limited capacity to carry nutrients (glucose, fats, oxygen) to the working muscles and to remove the by-products of metabolism (carbon-dioxide, heat and lactic acid). Although it is not possible to replace all the water lost in heavy sweating, even partial replacement can limit the problems of overheating and minimize the risk of circulatory collapse.

For longer runs such as marathon training or competition in hot and humid conditions, regular fluid intake is essential to prevent dehydration and the possibility of heat injury. The golden rule is *little and often*. Pyke and Sutton (1992) recommended small volumes (150–200ml) drunk regularly (every fifteen to twenty minutes).

If a runner attempts to replace too much water (without replacing lost electrolytes) a toxic state may develop known as hyponatraemia. (Noakes and Speedy, 2006; Noakes, 2012; Bruckner, 2013). This can result in headaches and convulsions because of swelling of brain cells and increased brain pressure. Partial replacement (40–50 per cent) of fluid should be adequate to reduce the risk of overheating and impairment of performance.

One of the key factors determining the rate of fluid replacement is stomach emptying. There are a number of 'sports' drinks commercially available. Most claim to be **isotonic**, suggesting that the mineral content (types and amounts), together with other dissolved solids, makes it in balance with the body's own fluids. Therefore the fluid consumed leaves the stomach easily and quickly to be absorbed in the intestines.

It is often claimed that sports drinks containing essential mineral salts (electrolytes) replace the mineral salts lost during heavy sweating. This may be true to some degree. However, Pyke and Sutton (1992) reported that electrolyte loss during heavy sweating is not great. Concentration of principal electrolytes in sweat, such as sodium and chloride, may be almost one-third that in plasma and therefore water is the most important substance to replace, but the inclusion of some electrolytes in the water may help absorption.

Carbohydrate concentration in the drink can affect stomach emptying. Carbohydrate content in **isotonic** sports drinks is usually only between 4 per cent and 7 per cent, which can be enough to provide a slight energy boost, but not enough to significantly slow down stomach emptying. In other words, there will be between 4 and 7g of carbohydrate per 100ml of fluid.

Hypotonic (less dense than the body's fluid) drinks are also useful during the event, being quickly absorbed and speeding up rehydration.

Hypertonic drinks are more concentrated than the body's own fluids and could contribute towards dehydration if used during performance. However, if they are hypertonic because of a large amount of carbohydrate they can be very useful for consuming immediately after an event when hydration, though important, is not necessarily as important as the intake of carbohydrate for glycogen repletion. It could be possible to take in sufficient carbohydrate in liquid form, whereas solid food may be difficult to face immediately after a vigorous event.

Dilute carbohydrate and electrolyte solutions are more effective as rehydrating agents than water alone because their electrolyte and glucose content increases the rate of water absorption across the small intestine (Williams, 1995).

For longer runs in hot and humid conditions fluid with between 2 and 7 per cent carbohydrate may be recommended, whereas in moderate to cold conditions fluid with between 10 and 16 per cent carbohydrate may be recommended.

Of great importance is to find what fluid/fuel suits you on training runs so that you can use this in a race, if this is your goal, and avoid using something in a race that you have not previously tried in training.

RUNNING IN LATER LIFE

It was once asked of the famous mountaineer, Chris Bonnington, why he climbed mountains. His short, sharp, rhetorical reply was, 'Because I can!' When people ask of me why I run, that same answer rings true: 'Because I can!'

Because we can, we do; because we do, we can. We enter a positive cycle, a positive upward spiral of health, fitness and vitality, whatever our age.

On the other hand, there can be a downward, negative spiral of decline and eventual infirmity should we allow it to happen: if we don't, we can't; if we can't, we don't.

There is no upper age limit to running. We are never too old. Nor is there an age when we should stop. How do we determine who is old? What is old age? How do we determine when old age is reached? Old means many things to many people. Some are 'old' before their time, while others remain young at heart, active and nimble well into their later years. Does old age begin with the big Four-O? They say life begins at forty, and so it should.

The next milestone is fifty. How many excellent fifty-plus athletes do I know who can out-run many a twenty-one-year-old! Does old age begin when we retire from work? Retirement certainly offers a dramatic change in lifestyle. That change could be positive and involve increased activity now that time and opportunity exists, or negative, a chance to sit, vegetate and atrophy.

Age is a fact of life; it is a chronological passing of years. Old is an attitude of mind. True,

the body ages. The ageing process causes deterioration of the body's tissues and their function, but although 'over the hill' at forty, this does not necessarily mean we are on the slippery slope to infirmity. Although we cannot prevent or reverse the ageing process, we can slow it down and reduce its effect. By remaining or becoming active in later life we can develop and maintain a considerable amount of strength, stamina and suppleness well beyond our prime.

Fig. 11.1   Running maintains a good level of aerobic capacity in later life.

After a peak in work capacity the tissues and systems of the body progressively deteriorate as we get older. Healthy older people lose strength (the ability to exert force) by about 1 to 2 per cent per year and power (force × speed) by about 3 to 4 per cent per year (Young and Dinan, 1996). For some older people there may come a time when they do not have enough strength to perform everyday tasks such as climbing stairs or rising from a chair unaided. By remaining active, or becoming active into later life, this deterioration can be reduced, especially the loss of muscle tissue, and an amount of strength can be maintained. Regular exercise increases strength, endurance and flexibility. In percentage terms, improvements seen in older people are similar to those in younger people (Young and Dinan, 1996).

Fitness, through the development and maintenance of the three 'S's (strength, stamina, suppleness), should be a way of life. Despite the natural ageing process and the inevitable deterioration of the body's systems, work capacity can be maintained well above a minimal threshold by remaining active into later life.

Exercise can also help to prevent certain conditions that affect people in middle age and later life such as coronary heart disease, stroke and osteoporosis. And let us not forget the social and psychological benefits of exercise. Running offers important opportunities for socialization; it helps us to meet people, whether an old or new friend, which in turn improves state of mind.

Running should not be viewed as self-inflicted pain, torture, masochism, or any of the other negative and degrading terms some people use. Like good food, or an excellent wine, running can be pleasurable, rewarding and satisfying, and can offer relief from stress. The body needs exercise; its systems thrive on exercise.

So don't let anybody say to you, 'You shouldn't do that sort of thing at your age!' They might not, but then they *may* not be capable of coping with the physical tasks of every-day life, let alone the pleasures of additional physical pursuits.

I have a friend and former GB Triathlon team member who competed in the World Triathlon Championships in Mexico the day after her seventy-first birthday. In that same sport, Patrick Barnes has become known and respected, participating into his mid-eighties. Another runner, Bill Synnott, completed our local half-marathon at the age of eighty-one; he didn't start running until he was seventy-nine. Madge Sharples was the oldest lady to run the original London Marathon and eventually wrote her book, *Marathon Madge, 71 and Still Running.*

Precautions in Later Life

The New Older Runner

At any age, a person wishing to take up running to improve his or her fitness would be advised to start off very gently. As we get older, this advice is even more important. We must also consider how much exercise we have done recently, if any. After a long period of comparative inactivity, we may not be able to just get up and go! The systems of the body may have degenerated with age and, through inactivity, will not be developed enough to cope with too high an overload.

For the older person new to running it may be advisable to develop a background of regular, good-pace walking. Regular walking will help to strengthen muscles and will improve aerobic capacity to a degree.

Eventually (and do not be impatient) we can progress to jogging. Start off walking, but intersperse the walk with short intervals of jogging. *Do not forget the importance of a correct-pace warm-up, and, most importantly for an older person, correct cool-down*, as discussed previously in this book. In addition, an amount of regular gentle stretching is important, also discussed previously in the book.

This regime may last a few weeks, but as our fitness increases (the body's systems adapt) the walking sections reduce in number and length and the jogging intervals increase in number and length.

As further adaptation occurs and fitness improves we will progress to jogging continuously for the whole of the session. However, do not get carried away with your enthusiasm. Remember that rest is an important part of any training regime and so restrict your runs to about three per week at the most for a while.

Hopefully, if you have been sensible and patient, you will reach this stage with no ill-effects, injury or trauma, other than normal physical reaction to the new and unaccustomed activity; there may be some tiredness (hence the rest days) and there may be some initial muscle ache. If muscles become too painful, you have overdone the running and will need a longer period of rest before the next session.

The Experienced Older Runner

Usually, when people have been running for quite a number of years, they appreciate the many physical, mental and social benefits afforded from the activity. Therefore it becomes a way of life and for a lifetime. There is no upper age limit, no age at which we are advised to stop.

However, as we age, the body's systems lose some degree of condition and are not quite as effective or efficient as when we were younger. We must accept that we cannot run as fast, or possibly as far, as we used to. We must also accept that if we tried to, we would increase our risk of injury.

Some people are content to continue to run for health-related fitness, while others still have a desire to race. Many performers over fifty and over sixty can still achieve very respectable times in races, beating runners ten and twenty years younger, and win age-group trophies. Others still enjoy 'racing' on road, fell or cross-country but accept they are not going to be in the prizes.

The majority are slower than they used to be and may realize that a longer rest period is required. As we get older the body takes longer to recover and we risk injury if we try to do too much without adequate rest and recovery. Rest may involve complete rest from running for a day, or a shorter, easier 'recovery' run may follow the day after a race.

With care and common sense, running can continue relatively injury-free well into later life. The benefits of running are numerous for people of all ages. With knowledge of technique, body structure and function, and the principles of training, it should be safe, effective and enjoyable.

Can you run the risk of not exercising, knowing that inactivity is more dangerous for the cardiovascular system than smoking, high blood pressure and diabetes? Even if you are unfortunate enough to have one or more of these conditions, you can still exercise, but take professional advice.

REFERENCES

American College of Sports Medicine (1986). *Guidelines for Exercise Testing and Prescription, 3rd Edition*, Lea & Febiger, Philadelphia. Chapter 2, 9-30; Appendix A, 145–146; Appendix C, 153–155.

Anderson, B. and Anderson, J. (2010). *Stretching*. Shelter Publications, Bolinas, California, USA.

Ashton, D. and Davies, B. (1986). *Why Exercise?* Basil Blackwell, Oxford.

Baird, J. (2006). *Running Fit*. Collins and Brown, London.

Bean, A. (1996). *The Complete Guide to Sports Nutrition* (second edition). A & C Black, London.

Bean, A. (1999). *Food for Fitness*. A & C Black, London.

Bonanno, J.A. and Lies, J.E. (1974). Effects of physical training on coronary risk factors, *American Journal of Cardiology*, 33: 760–764.

Brand-Miller, J. (1998). Carbohydrates. *Essentials of Human Nutrition*, Mann, J. and Truswell, A.S. (Eds). Oxford University Press, Oxford, England.

Bromley, P. (1998). Prevention of exercise related injuries, *Exercise*, The Exercise Association of England, Nov/Dec.

Brukner, P. (2013). Challenging beliefs in Sports nutrition: are two 'core principles' proving to be myths ripe for busting? Br J *Sports Med*, 47, 11, 663–664.

Brunner, D. and Manelis, G. (1960). Myocardial infarction among members of communal settlements in Israel, *Lancet*, Vol. 276, No. 7159: 1049–1050.

Burfoot, A. (Ed.). 2009. *Runners World Complete Book of Running*. Rosedale, USA.

Carlton, I. (2001). Optimize your energy stores with the 'glycaemic index', *Peak Performance*, 146 (March).

Chomistek, A.K., Lu, B., Sands, M., Going, S.B., Garcia, L., Allison, M.A., Stefanick, M.L., Sims, S.T., LaMonte, M.J., Johnson, K.C., Manson, J.E. and Eaton, C.B. (2012). Abstract 006: Relationship of sedentary behaviour and physical inactivity to incident coronary heart disease: Results from the Women's Health Initiative. *Circulation*, March, 125, 10, supplement.

Cullum, R. and Mowbray, L. (1989). Y.M.C.A. *Guide to Exercise to Music*. Pelham Books.

Curry, B.S., Chengkalath, D., Crouch, G.J., Romance, M. and Manns, P.J. (2009). Acute effects of dynamic stretching, static stretching, and light aerobic activity on muscular performance in women. *J Strength Cond Res*, Sept, 23, 6, 1811–1819.

Davis, D., Kimmet, T. and Auty, M. (1988). *Physical Education: Theory and Practice*. MacMillan Company of Australia, Melbourne.

Douglas, S. (2013). *The Runners World Guide to Minimalism and Barefoot Running*. Rosedale, USA.

Fox, S.M. and Haskell, W.L. (1968). Physical activity and the prevention of coronary heart disease, *Bulletin of the New York Academy of Sciences*, 44: 950–967.

Garber, C.E., Blissmer, B., Deschenes, M.R., Franklin. B.A., Lamonte, M.J., Lee, I.M.,

Nieman, D.C. and Swain, D.P. (2011). American College of Sports Medicine position stand: Quantity and quality of exercise for developing and maintaining cardiorespiratory, musculoskeletal, and neuromotor fitness in apparently healthy adults; guidance for prescribing exercise. *Med Sci Sports Exerc.* Jul, 43, 7, 1334–59.

Gielen, S. (2010). Exercise in cardiovascular disease. *Circulation*, September, 122, 12, 1221–1238.

Glover, R., Shepherd, J. and Glover, S-L. F. (1996). *The Runner's Handbook*. Penguin, New York.

Hamer, M., Ingle, L., Carroll, S. and Stamatakis, E. (2012). Physical activity and cardiovascular mortality risk: Possible protective mechanisms. *Med Sci Sports Exerc*, January, 44,1, 84–88.

Haskel, W.L., Lee, I-M., Pate, R.R., Powell, K.E., Blair, S.N., Franklin, B.A., Macera, C.A., Heath, G.W., Thompson, P.D. and Bauman, A. (2007). Physical activity and public health: Updated recommendation for adults from the American College of Sports Medicine and the American Heart Association. *Med Sci Sports Exerc*. August, 39, 8, 1423–1434.

Hoeger, W.W.K. and Hoeger, S.A. (2013). *Principles and labs for fitness and wellness* (12th Edition). Thompson Wadsworth, Belmont, Ca.

Honneybourne, J., Hill, M. and Moors, H. (1996). *Advanced Physical Education and Sport*. Stanley Thomas, Gloucestershire, England.

Jones, H. (2010). *How to Run*. Carlton Books, London.

Kay, A.D. and Blazevich, A.J. (2012). Effect of acute static stretch on maximal muscle performance: a systematic review. *Med Sci Sports Exerc*, Jan, 44 (1), 154–164.

Lycholat, T. (1995). Stretching methods. *Sports Industry*, 115 (Mar) 22–23.

Maughan, R.J. (1990). Marathon Running. *Physiology of Sports*, Reilly, T., Secher, N., Snell, P. and Williams, C. (Eds). E. & F.N. Spon, London.

McArdle, W.D., Katch, F.I. and Katch, V.L. (1991). *Exercise Physiology*. Lea and Febiger, Philadelphia.

McDougal, C. (2009). *Born To Run*. Profile Books, London.

McHugh, M.P. and Cosgrave, C.H. (2010). To stretch or not to stretch: the role of stretching in injury prevention and performance. *Scand J Med Sci Sports*, Apr, 20, 2, 169–181.

Mitchell, L. and Dale, B. (1980). *Simple Movement*. John Murray, London.

Morris, J.N. (1953). Coronary heart disease and physical activity of work, *Lancet*, Vol. 262, No. 6795: 1053–1057.

Morris, J.N. and Adam, C. (1973). Vigorous exercise in leisure-time and the incidence of coronary heart disease, *Lancet*, Vol. 301, No. 7799: 333–339.

Nelson, M.E., Rejeski, W.J., Blair, S.N., Duncan, P.W., Judge, J.O., King, A.C., Macera, C.A. and Castaneda-Sceppa, C. (2007). Physical activity and public health in older adults; recommendations from the American College of Sports Medicine and the American Heart Association. *Circulation*, August, 116, 9, 1094–1105.

Noakes, T.D. and Speedy, D.B. (2006). Case proven: exercise associated hyponatraemia is due to overdrinking. So why did it take 20 years before the original evidence was accepted?. *Br J Sports Med*. 40, 7, 567–572.

Noakes, T.D. (2012). Waterlogged: *The serious problem of overhydration in endurance sports*. Human Kinetics, Champaign, Illinois, USA.

Norris, C. (1994). *Flexibility Principles and Practice*. A & C Black, London.

Norris, C. (2008). *Stretching for Running*. A & C Black, London.

REFERENCES

Paffenbarger, R.S. and Hale, W.E. (1975). Work activity and coronary heart mortality. *New England Journal of Medicine*, 292, 11: 545–550.

Paffenbarger, R.S., Wing, A.L. and Hyde, R.T. (1978). Physical activity as an index of heart attack risk in college alumni. *American Journal of Epidemiology*, 108: 161–175.

Pearson, P. (1998). *Safe and Effective Exercise.* Crowood Press, Wiltshire.

Pope, R.P., Herbert, R.D., Kirwan, J.D. and Grantham, B.J. (2004). A randomized trial of pre-exercise stretching for prevention of lower-limb injury. *Med Sci Sports Exerc*, Feb; 32 (2), 271–277.

Pullig-Schaltz, M. (1994). Easy hamstring stretches. *The Physician and Sportsmedicine*, 22 (2), 115–116.

Pyke, F.S. and Sutton, J.R. (1992). Environmental Stress, *Textbook of Science and Medicine in Sport*, Bloomfield, J., Fricker, P.A. and Fitch, K.D., (Eds). Blackwell Scientific Publications, Victoria, Australia, 114–133.

Scheuer, J. and Tipton, C.M. (1977). Cardiovascular Adaptation to Physical Training. *Annual Review of Physiology*, 39: 221–251.

Sharkey, B.J. (1975). *Physiology and Physical Activity.* Harper & Row, New York.

Sharkey, B.J. (1990). *Physiology of Fitness.* Human Kinetics, Champaign, Illinois.

Smith, B. (1994). *Flexibility for Sport.* Crowood Press, Wiltshire.

Thacker, S.B., Gilchrist, J., Stroup, D.F. and Kimsey, C.D. Jr. (2004). The Impact of stretching on sports injury risk: a systematic review of the literature. *Med Sci Sports Exerc*, Mar, 36, 3, 371–378.

Warren, T.Y., Barry, V., Hooker, S.P., Sui, X., Church, T.S. and Blair, S.N. (2010). Sedentary behaviours increase risk of cardiovascular disease mortality in men. *Med Sci Sports Exerc.* May, 42, 5, 879–885.

Westaway, D. (1991). The new aerobic myth…slow down and burn more fat. *Pro Link*, (Dec/Jan).

Willett, G.M., Hyde, J.E., Uhrlaub, M.B., Wendel, C.L. and Karst, G.M. (2001). Relative activity of abdominal muscles during commonly prescribed strengthening exercises. *J Strength Cond Res*, Nov, 15, 4, 480–485.

Williams, C. (1990). Metabolic aspects of exercise. *Physiology of Sports*, Reilly, T., Secher, N., Snell, P. and Williams, C. (Eds). E. & F.N. Spon, London.

Williams. C. (1995). Nutrition, Energy Metabolism, and Ergogenic Aids; *ABC of Sports Medicine*, BMJ Publishing.

Woods, K., Bishop, P. and Jones, E. (2007). Warm-up and stretching in the prevention of muscular injury. *Sports Med*, 37, 12, 1089–1099.

Young, A. and Dinan, S. (1996). Fitness for older people. *Pro Link*, (April/May), 18–20. (Reprinted in *Pro Link* with permission from the *BMJ* [1994], 309, 331–333).

Zukel, W., Lewis, R.H. and Enterline, P. 1959). A short-term community study of the epidemiology of coronary heart disease, *American Journal of Public Health*, 49: 1630.

RECOMMENDED FURTHER READING

Marathon and Half Marathon Running, Steve Trew. Crowood Sports Guides – Skills, Techniques, Training, 2012.

Nutrition for Marathon Running, Jane Griffin. Crowood, 2005.

High Performance Long Distance Running, David Sutherland. Crowood, 2011.

Marathon and Half Marathon Training Guide, Graeme Hilditch. Crowood, 2007.

Improve your Marathon and Half Marathon Times, David Chalfen. Crowood, 2012.

Trail and Mountain Running, Sarah Rowell and Wendy Dodds. Crowood, 2013.

Off-Road Running, Sarah Rowell. Crowood, 2002.

Born To Run, Christopher McDougall. Profile Books, 2009 and 2010.

Lore of Running, Tim Noakes, MD. Human Kinetics, 4th Ed. 2002.

5k and 10k From Start to Finish, Graeme Hilditch. A & C Black, 2011.

Stretching for Running, Christopher M. Norris. A & C Black, 2008.

Running Repairs: A Runner's Guide to Keeping Injury Free, Paula Coates. A & C Black, 2007 (eBook, Bloomsbury, 2013).

Runner's World, Complete Book of Women's Running, Dagny Scott Barrios. Rodale, 2008.

Runner's World, The Runner's Body, Ross Tucker PhD and Jonathan Dugas PhD. Rodale, 2009.

Running Injuries: How to Prevent and Overcome Them, Tim Noakes and Stephen Granger. Oxford University Press, 2007.

GLOSSARY

Achievable maximum heart rate The fastest that an individual's heart can beat determined by a physical test where the performer exercises to maximum intensity.

Actin A protein filament which, in combination with a myosin filament, causes contraction of the muscle when stimulated by a nerve. The actin filament slides over the myosin filament.

Adaptation Long-term anatomical and physiological changes which occur in the tissues as a result of training.

Adenosine diphosphate (ADP) A chemical compound of one adenosine molecule and two phosphate molecules, which results from the breakdown of ATP during energy production. When combined with creatine phosphate (CP) resynthesizes ATP.

Adenosine triphosphate (ATP) A chemical compound of one adenosine molecule and three phosphate molecules stored in the muscles necessary for muscle contraction.

Adrenaline Hormone produced by the adrenal glands which stimulates heart action, relaxes bronchial tubes and other smooth muscle. Sometimes known as the 'fight or flight' hormone.

Aerobic With, or in the presence of, oxygen.

Aerobic fitness Ability to take in, transport, and utilize oxygen.

Age-related maximum heart rate Theoretically the fastest that a person's heart can beat as determined by subtracting the person's age from 220.

Ageing The reduction in work capacity, reduction in the efficacy of the systems of the body and the degeneration of tissues that naturally occurs as a person gets older after reaching a peak.

Agonist The muscle that contracts to cause a movement (prime mover).

Alveoli Tiny air sacs in the lungs surrounded by blood capillaries. Oxygen is transferred from the alveoli to the blood and carbon dioxide is transferred from the blood to the alveoli.

Amino acid Nitrogen-containing organic acid forming the building blocks of protein. There are 20 standard amino acids found in protein (in fact there are 23 'proteinogenic' AAs and about 500 AAs altogether).

Anatomy The science of the structure of the body.

Antagonist The muscle which lengthens to control a movement.

Anaerobic Without, or in the absence of, oxygen.

Anaerobic threshold (AT) Also known as Lactic Threshold; the level of exercise intensity whereby the production of energy switches from aerobic (with adequate oxygen) to anaerobic (without adequate oxygen) and lactic acid begins to accumulate in the muscles and the blood. Sometimes referred to as Lactate Threshold where blood lactate accumulation reaches 4mmol/l (see also OBLA).

Angina pectoris Pain in the chest, often felt during exertion or emotion, because of a heart disorder (lack of oxygen to the heart muscle).

Aorta The main artery of the body, which leaves the left ventricle of the heart.

Arteriosclerosis Hardening of the arteries, usually because of the effects of atherosclerosis.

Artery A blood vessel which carries oxygenated blood away from the heart.

Atherosclerosis Degeneration of arteries because of a build-up of fatty deposits (plaques) which results in a narrowing of the artery.

Atrium One of the two upper chambers of the heart which receives blood from the veins.

Atrophy Wasting of body tissue, from disuse, disease or lack of nutrition.

Blood pressure The pressure exerted by the blood on the artery wall resulting from the pumping action of the heart and the resistance to the flow of blood.

Bone density The strength of a bone that affects its ability to withstand stress.

Calorie Unit of energy, specifically heat energy. Large C (large Calorie or kilocalorie): the amount of heat required to raise the temperature of 1 kilogram of water through 1 degree Celsius. Small c (small calorie): the amount of heat required to raise the temperature of 1 gram of water through 1 degree Celsius. 1,000 small calories = 1kilocalorie (kcal) = 4.186 (4.2) kilojoules (kJ): NB: Usually, when referring to the calorie content of food, or calorie expenditure during physical activity, we refer to large Calories (kilocalories).

Capillary Microscopic blood vessels which communicate between the arterioles and the venules (the end of the arterial system and the beginning of the venous system). The walls are microscopically thin so that fluids can pass through.

Carbohydrate Food substance that is the main source of work energy. Organic compounds of carbon, hydrogen and oxygen broken down in the body to glucose; stored in the muscles and liver as glycogen.

Carbon dioxide (CO_2) A gas produced in the body as a waste product of energy production. It stimulates respiration and is carried by the blood to the lungs to be exhaled.

Cardiac Pertaining to the heart.

Cardiac output (Q) The volume of blood pumped by the heart per minute.

Cardiovascular Pertaining to the heart and circulatory system.

Cartilage Smooth, whitish tissue which covers the ends of bones at joints and is able to withstand pressure.

Central nervous system (CNS) The brain and spinal cord.

Cholesterol A type of blood fat produced by the liver. Cholesterol is necessary for normal functioning of the body, but high levels of cholesterol are associated with the development of heart disease.

Collagen Fibrous, relatively inelastic, protein which forms the fibres of connective tissue in tendons. Collagen connective tissue is also found in muscles.

Concentric contraction Muscle tension where the muscle shortens (the fibres shorten towards the centre).

Connective tissue Tissue in the body made up of collagen and elastin fibres (e.g. tendons, ligaments and fascia).

Coronary arteries Arteries supplying blood to the heart muscle. Usually referring to the arteries which originate from the aorta and supply the heart muscle with oxygen and nutrients.

Creatine phosphate A high-energy compound that assists in the resynthesis of adenosine triphosphate and the continuation of energy production in the muscle.

Dehydration Loss of essential body fluids, mainly water.

Delayed onset muscle soreness Muscle soreness that peaks approximately 24 to 48 hours after unfamiliar or vigorous exercise (particularly in muscles used eccentrically such as in the quadriceps after running downhill).

Diaphragm Sheet of muscle across the bottom of the rib cage which separates the thoracic cavity from the abdominal cavity and assists with the mechanical act of breathing.

Diaphysis The central shaft of a growing bone.

Diastole The relaxation phase of the heart muscle after contraction (systole).

Disc (intervertebral) Fibro-cartilaginous pad between the vertebrae.

Eccentric contraction Muscle tension where the muscle lengthens.

Endorphins Pain-relieving substances secreted by the body similar to the drug morphine.

Enzymes Chemical substances which cause reactions in the body and affect metabolic processes.

Elasticity (elastic) The degree to which a structure, when deformed, returns to its original shape or size.

Epiphysis The enlarged end of a growing bone.

Erythrocyte Red blood cell.

Extension Movement of a joint whereby two bones move away from each other. In simple terms, straightening of a flexed (bent) limb.

Epiphyseal/plate (growth plate) Cartilaginous section of a growing bone which separates the epiphysis from the diaphysis.

Extensor A muscle which extends a limb or body part.

Fascia Thin connective tissue separating compartments of the body or separating individual muscles.

Fibrinogen A protein manufactured in the liver and released into the blood to act as a clotting agent. It combines with thrombin to produce long threads of fibrin and helps blood to clot.

Fixator A muscle which fixes (stabilizes) a joint and holds it static.

Fixator synergist A muscle which assists the prime mover by stabilizing a joint which the prime mover would otherwise move.

Flexibility The range of movement (ROM) at joints.

Flexion Movement of a joint whereby two bones come towards each other. In simple terms, bending an extended (straightened) limb or body part.

Flexor A muscle which flexes a limb or body part.

Glucose The simplest form into which carbohydrate is broken down during digestion.

Glycogen Carbohydrate in its stored form in the muscles and the liver. A glucose polymer which can be converted to glucose for energy production.

Golgi Tendon Organ (GTO) A sensory device within the muscle which detects high tension in the muscle fibres, initiating a consequent relaxation of the muscle fibres.

Growth plate Cartilaginous section of a growing bone which separates the epiphysis from the diaphysis (main shaft of a bone). The part of the bone which continues to allow bone growth after the two ends (epiphyses) and the central shaft (diaphysis) have hardened (ossified).

Health-related fitness A level of fitness which maintains a healthy state in the body. Sometimes referred to as general fitness and involves the development of strength, stamina and suppleness.

Haemoglobin The red oxygen-carrying pigment in red blood cells.

Heart rate (HR) The number of heart beats per minute (bpm).

Heart rate range The difference between resting and maximal heart rate.

High density lipoprotein (HDL) A protein responsible for the transportation of fats in the blood, particularly triglyceride and cholesterol, but with lower levels of triglyceride and cholesterol than Low Density Lipoprotein (LDL) and a higher amount of protein. A higher level of HDL is believed to elicit protection against heart disease and may be increased by regular aerobic exercise.

GLOSSARY

Hormones Substances produced by the endocrine glands which control numerous body processes.

Hyper-extension Extreme extension of a limb or the spine, beyond the usual normal range.

Hyper-flexion Extreme flexion of a limb or the spine, beyond the usual normal range.

Hypertrophy The enlargement of an organ or body tissue as a result of training or disease. (Do not necessarily get increase in strength.)

Hypertonic (When referred to ingested fluids): Having a higher osmotic pressure than body fluids.

Hypoglycaemia Low blood sugar.

Hypotonic (When referred to ingested fluids such as sports drinks): Having a lower osmotic pressure than body fluids.

Inverse Stretch Reflex An involuntary (reflex) action whereby muscle fibres relax in response to high tension in the muscle.

Involuntary Not under conscious control.

Isometric contraction Tension develops in the muscle but there is no joint movement (static).

Isotonic contraction Tension develops (and remains unaltered) in the muscle, which results in joint movement (dynamic).

Isotonic (When referred to ingested fluids such as sports drinks): Having an osmotic pressure equal to body fluids.

Kilojoule Metric unit of heat energy (1 kilojoule = 0.238 [0.24] Calories/kilocalories).

Lactic acid A bi-product of anaerobic metabolism in the muscle.

Lateral Away from the mid-line.

Lever A device employed to overcome a resistance or to create speed and range of movement. A lever will involve a rigid bar, a pivot point (fulcrum) and an effort force. An efficient lever is one where less effort is required to overcome a greater resistance.

Ligament Connective tissue which joins bone to bone at joints.

Lipoprotein A protein responsible for the transportation of triglyceride and cholesterol in the blood.

Low density lipoprotein (LDL) A protein responsible for the transportation of fats in the blood, particularly triglyceride and cholesterol, but with higher levels of triglyceride and cholesterol than High Density Lipoprotein (HDL) and a moderate amount of protein. High amounts of LDL are associated with the development of coronary heart disease.

Maximum oxygen uptake (VO$_2$ Max) The maximum volume of oxygen that can be extracted from the atmosphere and taken up by the tissues of the body, usually expressed in litres of oxygen per minute (l/min), or millilitres of oxygen per kilogram of body weight per minute (ml/kg/min).

Medial Towards the mid-line.

Metabolism All physiological and biochemical reactions in the body which provide energy for movement and materials for growth and repair.

Mitochondria Part of a cell, (including those in muscles) which processes oxygen for the production of energy.

Myocardial infarction (MI) A heart attack.

Myocardium The heart muscle.

Motor Pertaining to movement.

Motor nerve A nerve that carries messages from the central nervous system.

Muscle spindle A sensory device within a muscle which detects changes of muscle fibre length.

Myoglobin A protein within the muscle cell which is very receptive to oxygen and extracts the oxygen from the blood.

Muscle tone The healthy state which exists between the muscle and its stimulating nerve and the resulting condition whereby the muscle is always in a state of partial contraction.

Muscular endurance the ability to sustain repeated muscle actions or maintain a single contraction at a given force over a long duration.

Muscular strength The ability of the muscle to generate force to overcome a resistance.

Myofibril Part of the muscle cell made up of many sarcomeres of actin and myosin filaments.

Myosin A protein filament which, in combination with the actin filament, causes contraction of the muscle when stimulated by a nerve.

Neuromuscular The combined function between the nervous system and the muscles.

Neurone Nerve cell.

Nutrient Essential substance in the diet necessary for energy production, growth, maintenance and repair of tissues.

OBLA Onset of blood lactate accumulation. Indicated by a measurement of 4 mmol/l.

Ossification Bone hardening or bone formation.

Osteoporosis The degeneration of bones because of reduction in bone mass. (Loss of calcium is osteomalacia.)

Overload The stress imposed on tissues by training which is higher than that to which the tissues are accustomed.

Over-training Training that can result in fatigue, injury, a suppressed immune system and poor performance because of inadequate rest and recovery and an inability of the body to adapt. Also considered as 'under recovery'.

Overuse (Should not be confused with overload): Excessive overloading of tissues through very high levels of exercise, training or competition resulting in break-down of tissues with inadequate rest for re-building, repair and strengthening of those tissues. Often results in injury.

Plasma The liquid part of blood.

Plasticity (plastic) The characteristic of a substance to change its shape when warm and not return to its original shape.

Prime mover A muscle which shortens to cause movement of a joint.

Proprioceptor A sensory device within muscles, tendons and joints which detects changes in position or length. Also in the inner ear to influence balance.

Proprioception The detection of changes in the position of the body, or of muscle fibre lengthening/shortening.

Proprioceptive Neuromuscular Facilitation (PNF) stretching A form of developmental stretching employing the stretch reflex and the inverse stretch reflex to allow further relaxation of the muscle fibres and further muscle lengthening.

Protein A complex chemical compound of amino acids forming the essential part of every living cell. In the diet, one of the essential food substances.

Respiration The process of taking air into the lungs, oxygen from that air entering the blood being transported to all tissue cells, being used for the production of energy, and the transfer of carbon dioxide from the tissues to the blood, which is then transported back to the lungs and exhaled.

Responses Short-term physiological changes which occur during exercise and which quickly return to normal after exercise (e.g. increase in heart rate, increase in respiration, increase in muscle temperature, sweating, etc.).

Sarcomere A number of protein filaments of actin and myosin grouped together. Many sarcomeres make up a myofibril.

Sarcopenia Age- or disease-related loss of muscle tissue.

Sensory nerve A nerve that carries messages to the central nervous system.

Stamina Cardio-respiratory endurance; the ability of the heart, lungs and circulatory system to supply an adequate amount of oxygen to the working muscles and therefore keep the activity going for longer periods of time.

Static contraction A muscle contraction where no movement of a joint occurs (see Isometric contraction).

Strength The force a muscle or group of muscles can generate.

Stretch reflex An involuntary (reflex) action of muscle fibres whereby they develop tension in response to rapid or forceful lengthening.

Stroke volume (SV) The volume of blood ejected by the heart per beat.

Suppleness A condition of the muscles whereby they are able to lengthen fully and therefore allow full range of movement at a joint.

Synergist A muscle which assists another muscle.

Synovial fluid The fluid secreted by the synovial membrane and which lubricates and nourishes the joint.

Synovial membrane A membrane within the joint capsule which secretes synovial fluid.

Systole Contraction of the heart muscle which ejects blood into the aorta (see also diastole).

Tapering Reduction in training (volume and intensity) prior to a competition in order to allow the tissues to fully recover and adapt in an attempt to peak for a competition.

Tendon Connective tissue, made of collagen, which connects muscle to bone.

Toxin A poison produced in the body.

True synergist A muscle which contracts to assist the prime mover in the movement of a joint.

Vein A blood vessel which carries deoxygenated blood towards the heart.

Vena cava The main vein which carries blood to the right atrium of the heart.

Voluntary Under conscious control.

Wind chill Cooling effect caused by wind.

INDEX